A CASUAL GUIDE TO THE

RECKLESS

A CASUAL GUIDE TO THE MUSIC OF BRYAN ADAMS

NEIL DANIELS

RECKLESS

A CASUAL GUIDE TO THE MUSIC OF BRYAN ADAMS

BY

NEIL DANIELS

NEIL DANIELS

A CASUAL GUIDE TO THE MUSIC OF BRYAN ADAMS

Reckless – A Casual Guide To The Music Of Bryan Adams

First edition published, 2014

ISBN-13: 978-1499387742

ISBN-10: 1499387741

Copyright Neil Daniels © 2014

Visit Createspace at *www.createspace.com*

Visit Neil Daniels at *www.neildanielsbooks.com*

All rights reserved. No part of this publication may be reproduced, stored in a retrieval system, or transmitted in any form or by any means, electronic, mechanical, photocopy, recording or otherwise, without prior written permission of the copyright owner. Nor can it be circulated in any form of binding or cover other than that in which it is published and without similar condition including this condition being imposed on a subsequent purchaser.

NEIL DANIELS

A CASUAL GUIDE TO THE MUSIC OF BRYAN ADAMS

CONTENTS

INTRODUCTION

FOREWORD BY DEREK OLIVER

PART ONE* – *THE MUSIC

BEFORE THE ALBUMS

BRYAN ADAMS

YOU WANT IT, YOU GOT IT

CUTS LIKE A KNIFE

RECKLESS

INTO THE FIRE

WAKING UP THE NEIGHBOURS

18 TIL I DIE

ON A DAY LIKE TODAY

ROOM SERVICE

11

PART TWO – MISCELLANEOUS

TIMELINE

ASSORTED REVIEWS

TRIVIA

BRYAN ADAMS IN HIS OWN WORDS

ROCK SCRIBES TALK BRYAN ADAMS

DISCOGRAPHY

AFTERWORD BY DAVE SCOTT

APPENDECIES

BIBLIOGRAPHY & SOURCES

ACKNOWLEDGEMENTS

DISCLAIMER

ABOUT THE AUTHOR

PUBLISHED BOOKS BY NEIL DANIELS

PRAISE FOR THE AUTHOR'S PREVIOUS WORKS

INTRODUCTION

Why a book on Bryan Adams? Well, because to my knowledge there has yet to be a book published in recent years that is exclusively about his music and I'm in the frame of mind that he deserves one. Sure, his recent music has a lot to be desired and I haven't truly enjoyed anything he's done in the studio since *18 Til I Die*, almost twenty years ago now but he remains one of the most energetic and brilliant live performers in the industry. I'm an avid fan of his earlier work: *Cuts Like A Knife* and *Reckless* are truly superb albums and *Into The Fire* remains vastly underrated, and if it wasn't for that dreaded song that we all know and tolerate (some tolerate it less than others), *Waking Up The Neighbours* would be another one of his finest outings but nevertheless it remains a kick-ass rock album.

Sadly, in the late '90s he lost his way, and though *On A Day Like Today* and *Room Service* have some brief moments of excellence, he's now firmly entered the realms of middle of the road music populated by such seasoned folks as Phil Collins, Sting and Eric Clapton.

There was one point in Adams career when he was heavier than Bon Jovi and that says something about both artists. Maybe I'm being a little harsh on Adams.

I just live in hope that he'll hook up with Bob Clearmountain or Mutt Lange and make a rock album we've all been waiting for. One can only dream.

My almost dislike of his two most recent albums *Room Service* and *11* have something to do with the fashion in which they were recorded. I'm not a fan of Adams and his musicians recording in separate rooms in different countries and emailing samples and verses and such back and forth until a song is finished. I much prefer a complete band unity in a studio hammering out verses and tracks for weeks or months until an album is completed. Hopefully Adams will go back to the old school approach on future albums. He's got the energy and the rock persona on the live stage yet not in the studio there clearly something is lacking.

Bryan Adams is one of the most successful Canadian singer-songwriters of all time. He rose to fame with *Cuts Like A Knife* before the release of his global breakthrough album *Reckless*, which Adams celebrated in 2014 with 30th Anniversary *Reckless* Tour.

His best known song remains the 1991 single '(Everything I do) I Do It For You' which was the lead song for the hit movie *Robin Hood: Prince Of Thieves*. It also happens to be one of the best-selling singles ever.

A CASUAL GUIDE TO THE MUSIC OF BRYAN ADAMS

Adams has won numerous nominations and awards throughout his career, including twenty Juno Awards nominations, fifteen Grammy Award nominations and five Golden Globe and three Academy Award nominations.

He's also won a Grammy for 'Best Song Written Specifically For A Motion Picture Or Television' and MTV, ASCAP, American Music and Ivor Novello Awards. He was handed the Governor General's Performing Arts Award in May 2010 for his thirty year contribution to the arts.

He has been awarded the Order Of Canada and the Order Of British Columbia for his contributions to music and philanthropy via The Bryan Adams Foundation. He is a well-known humanitarian and animal rights activist as well as a successful photographer. In January 2010 he received the Allan Waters Humanitarian Award.

Adams was inducted into the Hollywood Walk Of Fame in March 2011 after having been inducted into Canada's Walk Of Fame in 1998 and was inducted into the Canadian Music Hall Of Fame at Canada's Juno awards back in April 2006. Adams regularly crops up as one of the greatest rock artists of all time. In 2008, *Billboard* ranked him Number 38 in their poll of the 'All Time Top Artists' as part of the *Billboard* Hot 100 50th Anniversary Charts.

Thought he's never been a darling of the critics he's had incredible mainstream success and while his popularity may have waned in the US here remains an incredibly popular live act in Australia, Europe and here in the UK where his music is still often played and his shows sell out. His 2014 30th Anniversary *Reckless* Tour of the UK is staged in some of our biggest arenas from 10,000 to 20,000+ capacities.

This book is about the music with just a few small glimpses into his personal life. It is not a biography, though, but rather, as the title suggests, a guide to his music; a whistle stop tour of his career.

Adams does not get written about often so here's my chance to talk about some of the most popular rock tunes of the last thirty or so years.

Similarly to be previous book in the series, *Electric World – A Casual Guide To The Music Of Journey's Neal Schon*, this book offers a potted guide to Bryan Adams' music. As it is 'A Casual Guide' it is by no means definitive but it should make a handy companion to my Neal Schon book and any other book on AOR and melodic rock.

Thank you to my fellow rock fans and writers who have offered some of their opinions to this book notably Derek Oliver – a legend in AOR/melodic rock circles – and to *Fireworks* Reviews Editor Dave Scott who contributes his own thoughts as well as many of the photos in the book.

Reckless explores his music (mostly leaving his personal life out of it!) and legacy and offers titbits of information and trivia about his various non-music projects but on the whole this handy little book is about the music of Bryan Adams.

Neil Daniels

www.neildanielsbooks.com

A CASUAL GUIDE TO THE MUSIC OF BRYAN ADAMS

NEIL DANIELS

FOREWORD BY

DEREK OLIVER OF *CLASSIC ROCK PRESENTS AOR*

Why do I like Bryan Adams?

For me that's an easy question to answer. I like him because he has one of the greatest rock 'n' roll voices of all time. It's similar to a blast-furnace frenzy with the wind whipping the flames half way around the factory. I think I described it once as like somebody sticking a firecracker down Rod Stewart's throat and getting him to front AC/DC. But that was the good old days, the anything can happen formative years before he went supernova with the house wives and the lonely hearts club bagging the world's longest chart run for fourteen weeks via the Number 1 single '(Everything I Do) I Do It For You'. Back then that sort of statistic actually meant something.

As a long standing hardcore record collector I first heard about Bryan as a teenager when he fronted Canadian pop band Sweeney Todd. Their *If Wishes Were Horses* album turned up in my local used store – it looked good with a thick gatefold cover but the music was hardly earth shattering. In fact it was clearly diabolical but that didn't stop me from noting this young man's name. As the years rolled by I saw him turning up as co-writer (normally with fellow Canadian Jim Vallance) on several tracks from some of my favourite hard rock bands. He had turned his hand to writing a slew of the catchiest hooks this side of Russ Ballard. Notable triumphs included the Teaze classic 'Boys Night Out', April Wine's 'You Could've Been A Lady', and other equally impressive stuff from the likes of Prism, Loverboy, Nantucket, Scandal and Uriah Heep. Later of course he'd end up with by-lines on much bigger metal monsters like KISS and Mötley Crüe.

The lad was on fire as a songsmith and then came the appearance of a couple of solo albums which sounded nice and dandy as pop rocking records often do. It wasn't until album number three that the world and myself really stood up and took notice. *Cuts Like A Knife* delivered on every count – vocally, musically and song wise. Bryan had found his voice, literally as it happened, carving out a distinct style and swagger that set him up for the monster twelve million selling (and counting) album *Reckless* resplendent with a shot of six hit singles. It was a record that not only defined him but also defined the era and, unlike many artists of his kind, it failed to stunt future growth allowing him to build and craft a career across many continents and musical genres.

Sadly, Bryan's hard rock defences were breached when further records moved further and further away from the very thing that first attracted me to him. Sure, there were moments when it looked like he'd rekindled the fire, most notably on the Mutt Lange produced 'The Only Thing That Looks Good On Me Is You', a fine low slung rocker with a suitably hoarse vocal and cheeky lyrics. Apart from that his hard rock credentials ebbed away to find another audience, one that supported ballads and tear-jerkers far more than the loud cock-rocking of his youth. Sadly, creatively speaking, this is the moment I waved goodbye to Bryan but who knows one day he might surprise me by cranking up his Telecaster, dousing his larynx with gasoline and knocking us out with an effortless riff and anthemic hook line.

Derek Oliver

Classic Rock Presents AOR / Rock Candy Records

London, July, 2014

A CASUAL GUIDE TO THE MUSIC OF BRYAN ADAMS

PART ONE

THE MUSIC

BEFORE THE ALBUMS

"Music became my focus. At 13, I was jamming with my mates. At 15, I was playing clubs".

- Speaking to Adrian Thrills, *Daily Mail*, 2008

Bryan Guy Adams was born in Kingston, Ontario to British folks Captain Conrad J. Adams and Elizabeth Jane Adams (nee Watson) who had immigrated to Canada from the UK in the 1950s. Adams' middle name derives from the British conspirator Guy Fawkes who was executed for an attempt to blow up the houses of Parliament in 1605, which consequently resulted in Guy Fawkes Day in England on November 5.

Conrad was a Sandhurst officer who joined the Canadian Army before being employed as a United Nations peacekeeping observer and subsequently a Canadian service diplomat. His mother, Elizabeth, was a schoolteacher and librarian. Adams was fortunate enough to get to travel with his parents on various diplomatic postings throughout Europe in the 1960s and the Middle East in the early 1970s travelling far and wide to such places as the UK, Austria and finally Portugal where he lived from 1969 to 1971. The family moved back to Ottawa from Portugal before relocating to Tel Aviv.

He spoke to *FT Magazine*'s Hester Lacey about this period: "They were mostly missionary schools with heavy religious overtones – the Church of Scotland School in Jaffa or St Columban's American School in Lisbon".

Uninterested in school, it was in Israel when his parents sent him to see a psychiatrist. "Dr Kaplan: very nice fellow", he admitted to *The Daily Telegraph*'s David Jenkins in 2008. "And one day he said to me, 'You know, Bryan, you're not the one who should be here; it's your parents who should be here'. And I realised that perhaps it was true. Quite liberating, in a sense: it gave me confidence that I was OK. And that was cool".

The family settled back in Canada after Adams refused to enroll at the military school Sandhurst in England which father and grandfather attended. His parents divorced and Adams lived with his mother and younger brother in Ottawa before moving permanently to Vancouver.

Adams got a job as a dish washer aged fourteen which provided him with enough cash to purchase his first guitar.

"I grew up with British rock", he told the *Daily Mail*'s Adrian Thrills in 2008. "I was into Joe Cocker and Rod Stewart, and that led me on to Ray Charles, Sam Cooke and the blues".

A CASUAL GUIDE TO THE MUSIC OF BRYAN ADAMS

With a guitar at hand he began auditioning for guitarists slots in local bands as well as rehearsing with his own outfit in the basement of his mother's rented home in North Vancouver. Adams couldn't find a singer for his band so he opted to sing himself which got him noticed by local musicians.

"We put ads in papers, all kind of things, trying to find a singer, and no one pitched up", he told *The Daily Telegraph*'s David Jenkins. "And I had, er, elected myself as the vocalist during rehearsals. And... and that was all there was to it".

He ended up in Shock by the age of sixteen and the glam rock band Sweeney Todd which he successfully auditioned for in the summer of 1976. The band had just had a hit in Canada with 'Rocky Roller' before losing their singer Nick Gilder.

Glam rock had arguably passed its peak years by this point having seen the rise of such artists as David Bowie, Queen, Slade, The Sweet, Roxy Music and T-Rex et al. All of them London based. The English capital was now undergoing a major cultural revolution with punk rock spearheaded by Sex Pistols, The Clash, The Damned and others.

Adams quit school to be in the band full time and he convinced his mum to use his college funds to buy him a Baby Grand piano.

The band got him to record new vocals for 'Roxy Roller' so they could reissue the single via London Records, the now legendary label which kick-started ZZ Top's career. The single entered the *Billboard* Hot 100 at Number 99 on September 18, 1976.

The band toured in support of their second album *If Wishes Were Horses*, released in August 1977, and included three Adams co-written tracks: 'Until I Find You', 'Pushin'' and 'Shovin''. His co-composer was bassist Budd Marr. Adams also co-wrote 'Song For A Star' with keyboardist Dan Gaudin. His tenure in the band did not last long as he quit in December 1977. It was more than clear by this point that Adams had a knack for writing a catchy tune.

Confident of his talents Adams did not go back to school and opted to go on the road and play nightclubs and bars. On his return to Canada he immersed himself in the Vancouver studio scene and was employed as a vocalist for the CBC and working under the tutelage of keyboardist Robbie King whom Adams has attributed as his first paid session gig.

A pivotal encounter came in January 1978 when he met Jim Vallance through a mutual friend at a Vancouver music store.

Vallance was working solo as a studio musician and songwriter after having quit the band Prism as their drummer and principal songwriter writing under the pseudonym Rodney Higgs.

Vallance did not take comfortably to touring and quit the band to attempt to forge a career as a songwriter and producer. Vallance and Adams arranged a meeting at Vallance's home studio a few days later which was the start of their long and very successful musical partnership.

It has been claimed that the duo sold songs to a variety of established artists to launch Adams' own solo career when in actual fact many of those songs were recorded after Adams had begun making his own albums.

Another important event happened in 1978 when later in the year Adams signed to A&M Records for the grand sum of one dollar.

Adams and Vallance had been sending demos to Canadian music labels since they met. In August they had signed a songwriting and production deal with the A&M publishing arm, Irving-Almo Music. Adams had actually begun talks with RCA Victor Records for a separate recording contract but A&M signed him on as a solo artist as they'd heard about his solo endevours.

It was around this time when Adams started to cut some demos, including 'I'm Ready' which appeared on his breakthrough North American album *Cuts Like A Knife*, and 'Remember' which ended up on his self-titled debut album. Ironically, both songs were covered by other artists before his own debut album was released. 'I'm Ready' appeared on the 1979 album *Goose Bumps* by Ian Lloyd formally of Stories.

Other songs that he recorded in the late 1970s include the disco track 'Let Me Take You Dancing' (with the B-side 'Don't Turn Me Away') which made the Canadian RPM chart in February/March 1979.

Adams has since disowned the track, though it was rather successful with twenty-three weeks spent in the *Billboard* dance charts and a reported 240,000 copies were sold. It peaked at Number 22.

'Straight From The Heart' was also recorded around this time before his first album was released. It first appeared on his third album, the aforementioned *Cuts Like A Knife*. The single would be a Top 10 US hit in 1983.

The third Prism album *Armageddon* also featured songs by Vallance and Adams who also collaborated with Prism guitarist Lindsay Mitchell on 'Jealousy'. He also wrote 'You Walked Away Again'.

Already Adams was crafting many songs and working towards his debut album.

BRYAN ADAMS

"The really early ones. They were part of the learning experience to be able to write the songs that everyone knows now. You need to learn to crawl before you walk".

- Speaking to Carl Weiser, *Song Facts*, 2009

Bryan Adams was released in February 1980 and was the first official release of the famed Adams-Vallance partnership which would continue to flourish well into the 21st Century.

The album was not initially released in the US. Most of the album was recorded in Manta Studios in Toronto between October 29 and November 29, 1979 with Adams and Vallance co-producing. It was then mixed at Sunset Sound by Bobby Schaper with some additional recording at Pinewood Studios by Geoff Turner and Alan Perkins.

Only the tracks 'Remember' and 'Wastin' Time' were not recorded during this time. The former was actually written for Bachman-Turner Overdrive and features on their 1979 opus *Rock 'N' Roll Nights* which was produced by Vallance. The latter was credited to Sweeney Todd guitarist Skip Priest and the band's manager/producer Martin Shaer but on the album it is credited to Adams as songwriter.

The album's first single was 'Hidin' From Love' (written with folk singer Eric Kagna) which peaked at Number 43 on the *Billboard* dance charts while 'Give Me Love' made it to Number 91 on the Canadian *RPM* 100 Singles chart.

Former Stories singer Ian Lloyd released *3WC* (*Third Wave Civilization*) in 1980 which featured two Adams/Vallance tracks that Adams would later record himself, 'Lonely Nights' and 'Straight From The Heart'.

Speaking about the genesis of the song, Adams spoke to *Song Facts*' Carl Weiser in 2009: "I wrote it when I was 18 and it was one of the first complete songs I'd ever written. I'd been living in Vancouver and teaching myself piano and this came out. Sometime after I had written the song, my friend Bruce Fairbairn was producing an album for an artist called Ian Lloyd, and wanted the song for him".

Mike DeGagne wrote on *All Music*: "Made up of brisk, pop-perky guitar fair, Bryan Adams' first album gained a considerate amount of airplay in Canada, but his notoriety abroad was still a couple of albums away. At 21, Adam's voice sounds a whole lot younger than his age, but the album itself holds up well, comprised of simple but buoyant pop songs".

Bryan Adams opens with 'Hidin' From Love' which is a pretty generic AOR track but it's some steady drums, a catchy rhythm and a dulcet melody. Adams' vocals are on form and the chorus is duly memorable. 'Win Some Lose Some' is a slightly heavier mid-paced track and Adams sings with a bit more gusto while 'Wait And See' is more of a guitar-based hands-in-the-air kind of track. 'Give Me Your Love' is a mid-album ballad that's not too far away from anything AOR stalwarts Styx or REO Speedwagon were churning out at the time. You can vision hands swaying in the air and lighters raised in the arena. 'Wastin' Time' picks up the pace with a strong riff and some steady drumming. Adams sings with confidence during 'Remember' which is a soulful melodic rock number aided by some groovy backing vocals; it's a number influenced by the Detroit R&B and motown sound. 'State Of Mind' is probably the album's standout track and still fondly thought of by fans. It's fast, sharp and polished with a nifty sing-along chorus. The closing number 'Try To See It My Way' opens with a piano riff before Adams joins in with some drums and bass courtesy of his fellow musicians. It's hardly the most invigorating song to finish the album.

  Overall, *Bryan Adams* is pretty lightweight stuff with some AOR clichés and obvious tricks of the genre. It was only a taster of bigger and better things to come. He was refining his sound.

  Bryan Adams was a minor success and eventually went Gold in Canada in 1986 by which time Bryan Adams had become a household name. His husky vocals, energetic stage presence, good looks and humble regular-guy attitude won him many fans and admirers around the world.

He formed a backing band in May 1980 and launched a tour of Canadian clubs and colleges for four months during which time he penned material for his second album.

Some of the album's songs were later covered by other artists: 'Hidin' From Love' and 'Remember' were covered by Rosetta Stone, a British outfit. The latter track actually made it to Number 46 on the Canadian *RPM* 100 Singles chart. The band Scandal covered 'Win Some, Lose Some' for their debut EP which was released in 1982. It was released as a single (the third release from the album) though it failed to chart.

Finally, in 1983 Bachelor Of Hearts covered 'A State Of Mind' for their opus *On The Boulevard* which features Ian Mitchell of Rosetta Stone and Bay City Rollers.

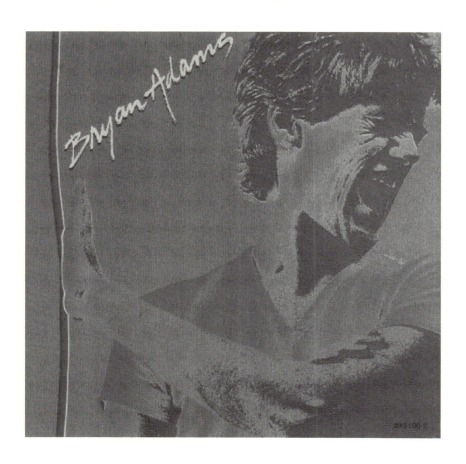

A CASUAL GUIDE TO THE MUSIC OF BRYAN ADAMS

YOU WANT IT, YOU GOT IT

"I'm sure that if you could snap your fingers and make every song a timeless one you would, but were there certain things while you were recording it that stood out?"

- Speaking to Dominick A. Miserandino, *The Celebrity Café*, 2008

Adams' second full-length studio opus *You Want It, You Got It* was recorded in early 1981 at Le Studio, Morin Heights, Quebec and was the first album co-produced by the much revered Bob Clearmountain who also engineered and mixed the recordings. The album cemented the classic Bryan Adams sound. It was recorded live in the studio with a band unlike the first album where Adams and Vallance played most of the instruments themselves.

The album includes Mickey Curry on drums, Jamie Glaser on guitars, Tommy Mandel on keyboards, organ and synthesizer, Jimmy Maelen on percussion, G.E. Smith on guitars Brian Stanley on bass, Jonathan Gerber on saxophone and Cindy Bullens performing background vocals while Adams sings, plays guitar and keys.

It was later mastered by the esteemed Bob Ludwig throughout a two week period in New York.

It was originally slated to be called 'Bryan Adams Hasn't Heard Of You Either' in cheeky reference to the reviews his self-titled debut but his recorded company noted for a more marketable title.

Released in 1981, it gave birth to the hit FM track 'Lonely Nights'. The song was a hit on the North East of the US were it gained airplay by late night broadcasters in such vicinities as Rochester, Albany and Syracuse. It helped gain him notice from other DJs, journalists and promoters in their US where he soon began playing clubs and hour long gigs for radio stations. 'Lonely Nights' was his first solo Hot 100 hit reaching Number 84 and Number 3 on the Mainstream Rock Chart.

You Want It, You Got It begins with 'Lonely Nights', an anthemic mid-paced rock ballad and a definite indicator of the sort of direction Adams would steer towards in his career. There's a decent guitar solo mid-song, too. 'One Good Reason' is an odd track and slightly out of place or at least too early in the track listing. There's something about it that doesn't gel with the rest of the album but the musicianship is pretty good, though. Adams gives it his all during 'Don't Look Now' which is a steady, honest rock number. 'Coming Home' is a paint by numbers ballad but Adams sings it with vehemence. 'Fits Ya Good' is an air guitar track with a sturdy riff and some toe-tapping sticks. 'Jealousy' is reminiscent of Springsteen circa 1975/76 with sprinklings of piano. It's an above average track, actually, and one that is seemingly forgotten about, sadly. 'Tonight' is another ballad which may seem like overkill as the album screams out for some more rock numbers but Adams has a fondness for mid-paced love songs. 'You Want It, You Got It' speeds things up and while the drums are too pronounced, the keys, bass and guitars keep the track afloat. There's some pretty strong guitar work but the production seems a little off. 'Last Chance' is a standard melodic rock track; it's catchy, though. The final track, 'No One Makes It Right', is a ballad but one of the album's better songs. It shows a different side to Adams voice and works a charm.

You Want It, You Got It, is a step up in terms of musicianship and production but it lacks some truly standout songs. The songwriting is stronger than on his first album and his voice sounds more mature but the riffs are missing. Rock albums are all about the riffs.

Adams also picked up some support slots for The Kinks and Foreigner after he started a six month tour of American in October.

"I've enjoyed it", he said to Gary James of *Classic Bands* in 1982 about touring with The Kinks. "It's been a real challenge for us because the Kinks' audiences are a very devout lot. I recently found out about the tour through our management and I left it in their hands to secure the dates. I didn't find out actually until three days before we were supposed to play with them".

'Coming Home' was also released as a single and was his debut Canadian Top 40 hit while 'Fits Ya Good' was also released.

Adams supported Loverboy on a tour of Canada in the spring of 1982. With the tours of the US and Canada and the radio success of some songs the album finally broke the *Billboard* chart in January 1982 when it hit Number 118.

Overall the album was a modest success but Adams' breakthrough release was yet to come. It was his concerts that suddenly gained him notice.

Such was Adams' knack for penning memorable FM tunes that during this time he wrote songs for a number of artists, including 'No Way To Treat A Lady' for Bonnie Raitt, 'Don't Let Him Know' for Prism, 'Teacher Teacher' for 38. Special and 'Edge Of A Dream' for Joe Cocker, amongst others.

As with the first album some of the songs were covered by other artists: Prism cut a version of 'Jealousy' while 'Tonight' was covered by Randy Meisner and 'Fits Ya Good' was covered by Tove Naess.

The songwriting duo of Adams and Vallance continued to pen songs for other arrests despite the release of Adams debut album.

Adams wrote 'Jump' with Paul Dean for the Loverboy album *Get Lucky* which was released in October 1981.

In January 1982 Prism released their fourth album *Small Change*.

It features the Adams/Vallance penned tracks 'Don't Let Him Know', which hit Number 1 on the Mainstream Rock Chart and was a Top 40 success on the Hot 100, and 'Stay'.

It was around this time when Adams begun writing for his next album. They were a fantastic team that complementing each other's talents. Vallance certainly helped nurture Adams growing songwriting skills. Vallance is an excellent keyboardist, drummer, bassist and guitarist as well as a talented songwriter. He taught Adams how to collect and refine his ideas. They wrote dozens of songs together and every now on them hit upon a real gem.

"If it hadn't happened for me in music, I would have been tenacious in something else", Adams admitted to *Reverb Online*'s Courtney Laura. "Who knows. I always wanted to be in music, maybe I'd have been a roadie. I don't think I would have been able to do the photography at the level I'm doing it now, because I would not have been able to afford it".

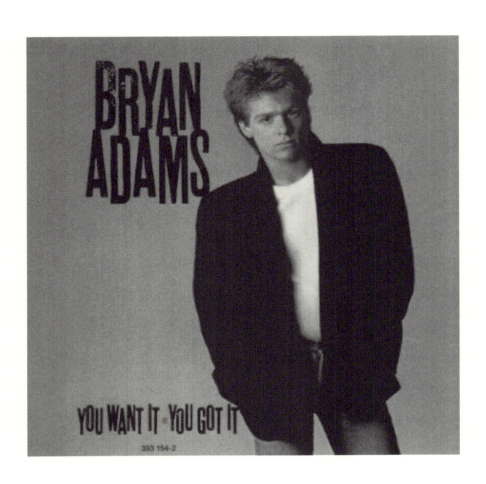

A CASUAL GUIDE TO THE MUSIC OF BRYAN ADAMS

CUTS LIKE A KNIFE

"With Jim [Vallance] we crawled from nothing, in a basement full of cat-piss, to write a collection of classic pop songs. It was the best ride of my life".

- Speaking to Dale Kawashima, *Songwriter Universe*, 2013

Produced by Bob Clearmountain and Adams, *Cuts Like A Knife*, was recorded and mixed between August 13 and October 20, 1982 at Little Mountain Sound, Vancouver, Canada. It was mixed at Le Studio, Morin-Heights, Canada.

'Straight From the Heart', which was originally written back in 1978 when he was eighteen years-old, was the last track recorded for the album and its title derived by Adams' folk singer buddy Eric Kagna. As previously mentioned it was first recorded by Ian Lloyd (formally of Stories) in 1980 on his *Third Wave Civilization* album while 'I'm Ready' was also first recorded by Lloyd for his solo opus *Goose Bumps* with Vallance on drums.

Adams was not enthusiastic about including 'This Time' but eventually made the final cut at Clearmountain's insistence. The recording sessions included the track 'Don't Leave Me Lonely' written with the late

KISS drummer Eric Carr which was intended for inclusion on the 1982 KISS album *Creatures Of The Night*, but failed to make the final cut.

Adams had been working with KISS on the 1982 compilation *Killers* before he relocated to Canada to work on his own album. *Creatures Of The Night* includes the track 'War Machine' which was written by Adams and Vallance with Gene Simmons.

Jim Vallance played percussion, electric piano on 'The Best Was Yet To Come' while the sessions included Mickey Curry on drums, Tommy Mandel on organ and synthesizer, Keith Scott on guitars and vocals, Dave Taylor on bass guitar, Alfa Anderson on background vocals and Lou Gramm of Foreigner on background vocals.

For the title-track Adams and Vallance were inspired by the melodies and chord progressions of such songs as 'Hey Jude' by The Beatles, 'Na Na Hey Hey Kiss Him Goodbye' by Steam and 'Love', Touchin', Squeezin'' by Journey.

Jim Vallance told the Vancouver newspaper *Georgia Straight* in 1988 about the origins of the album's title: "I think that I'm one of the world's best mumblers, I can mumble some of the best lyrics, but putting them together is another story. I think that's where Jim is really good – he can piece a story together. It's just a good thing to have the tape rolling when you're recording me. The best example was when we wrote

'Cuts Like A Knife', which was just literally a mumble. We looked at each other, rolled the tape back, and it sounded like 'cuts like a knife', so we started singing that".

It was released in January 1983 by A&M Records. The album spawned several hit singles, notably 'Straight From The Heart' which was the most successful and made the US Top 10 after its December 1982 release. The album's title-track made the US Top 15 and became one of Adams most popular songs while though it failed to chart in Europe 'This Time', the album's third released single, made the *Billboard* Hot 100 and was his first song to chart in Europe making it to Number 41 in the UK in 1986. Each single had an accompanying music video and would help launch his career and thus enter mainstream popularity.

The album's title-track remains by far the most successful and indelible song from the album. It received heavy airplay and was a regular fixture in the setlist. The music video for 'Cuts Like A Knife' was directed by Steve Barron, an Irish bloke, and filmed at an empty indoor swimming pool in Hollywood. It had been out of use and drained of water for years and also provided the location for Adams' platinum album party.

Both 'Straight From The Heart' and 'Cuts Like A Knife' were nominated for Juno Awards for 'Song Of The Year' while the latter would win Adams the 'Composer Of The Year' award.

The album itself peaked at Number 8 in the *Billboard* 200 album charts and went Platinum three times in Canada and the US while Down Under it went Gold. It did not fare so well outside of North America, though. However, after his global hit *Reckless*, *Cuts Like A Knife* would chart in the UK and be certified Silver.

Errol Somay wrote in *Rolling Stone*: "Refusing to look either forward or backward and drawing from limited sources, *Cuts Like A Knife* simmers in its own sameness. Which doesn't mean that stardom isn't imminent for this golden boy; in fact, this record is bland precisely because it grooms Adams for mass-market acceptance so shamelessly".

All Music's Eduardo Rivadavia later wrote: "Side one of this album is simply perfect… Side two opens with a few misfires, but recovers soon enough thanks to the gutsy guitar of 'Don't Leave Me Lonely' and the rather saccharine (but still good) ballad 'The Best Was Yet To Come'. Adams would finally achieve chart-topping perfection on his next release *Reckless*, but *Cuts Like A Knife* comes pretty close".

Cuts Like A Knife commences with 'The Only One', a finely crafted pop-rock number with a strong mid-song riff. 'Take Me Back' begins with a groovy riff before the drums and rhythm guitars and bass kick in. Adams handles the song expertly and the lyrics are strong. 'This Time' is a terrific rock track – perfect mid '80s melodic rock fodder. It seems timeless and a joy to listen to. 'Straight From The Heart' is one of

Adams' best known songs and needs little description. It's a delicate, moving ballad and Adams is absolutely superb. 'Cuts Like A Knife' is just about the perfect Bryan Adams song – lyrically and musically. It never ceases to raise a smile. 'I'm Ready' kicks into action and offers a truly infectious chorus. 'What's It Gonna Be' and 'Don't Leave Me Lonely' are both fine rock songs with some killer guitar work while 'Let Him Know' is an above average ballad and the final song 'The Best Was Yet To Come' brings to the album to a fixing climax, though, rock albums tend to have a more lasting impact when they close with rock songs rather than ballads but Adams handles it well.

Cuts Like A Knife is almost the perfect Bryan Adams album – a decent mix of rock songs and ballads with expert production, lyrics and musicianship. It still holds up after all this time.

Cuts Like A Knife remains one of this finest albums and was ranked Number 48 in the Top 100 Canadian Albums by Bob Mersereau in his tome. It was undoubtedly one of the most enduring albums of the decade and one of his greatest achievements.

Some of the tracks from the album were recorded by other artists, Notably 'Straight From The Heart' by Bonnie Tyler which features on her album *Faster Than The Speed Of Night*. Her version reached Number 45 in the US in May 1983. 'The Best Was Yet To Come' was covered by Laura Branigan in 1990 for her self-titled album.

'Straight From The Heart' was also covered by Rosetta Stone in 1982 and released as a single in November just a month before Adams released it himself. Ironically, 'I'm Ready' would be a hit for Adams years later after its inclusion on the 1997 album *MTV Unplugged*. It was also reissued in 2001 in Italy with lyrics by Zucchero Fornaciari and a new title, 'Io Vivo (In Te)'.

Adams spoke to Joe Bosso of *Music Radar* in 2010 about using the harmonica on the track: "I think I'm an OK harp player. I can certainly dig in. I've been playing harmonica since the '70s. I first recorded it in '81 on my second album. It's always an adventure, the harmonica – you never know where you're going to end up. It's a funny thing, though: it's a simple instrument to play, but simple and good are two different things!"

Adams enjoyed reinterpreting his own songs. The two versions of 'I'm Ready' are almost entirely different songs and the one thing he has learning about songwriting is that there is more than one way to consider a song. Songs need time to mature, to grow. Playing a song live is a good way to allow to song to evolve.

Adams launched his first headlining tour which kick-started in Canada and by the end of five months he had already performed over 100 gigs which helped make his name as a touring workhorse.

His band consisted of the late drummer Frankie LaRocka (who did not feature on the album) and keyboardist Johnny "Blitz" Hannah.

Adams supported Supertramp on their North American tour before flying to Vancouver to play in from of 30, 000 fans.

He was on the road in the US from March to August where he opened for the AOR band Journey. He later performed a six week solo tour of Europe which included a gig broadcast for German TV and radio as part of the revered *Rockpalast* series.

A solo tour of Japan was launched in November 1983 and supported The Police on a tour of Australia and New Zealand. All in all Adams played close to 300 live shows.

1983 was a hell of a busy year and his schedule would continue to be crazily busy. His greatest album was just around the corner.

RECKLESS

"Technically, I'm a hack. I don't fuss around with knobs and buttons and amplifiers. I go and plug in. My total theory of what I do is good feel. I feel it. I couldn't tell you the difference between a fader and a volume button. But I sure could tell you if I like it or not".

- Speaking to Gary James, *Classic Bands*, 1982

Adam's fourth album, *Reckless*, was co-produced by Adams and Bob Clearmountain.

Adams had begun recording the album in March 1984 after the *Cuts Like A Knife* World Tour but took a month's vacation after being unhappy with the recording process. He then returned to the studio in August to cut 'It's Only Love' with Tina Turner who at the time was making a huge comeback as a solo artist with *Private Dancer*. The song sparked rumours that the two had a relationship.

Adams, more enthused, began writing and recording new songs which would become the likes of 'Summer Of '69', 'Heaven' and 'Run To You'. The latter was originally written Blue Öyster Cult, but the group turned it down.

'Summer Of '69' had two primary influences: Vallance was inspired by the Jackson Browne song 'Running On Empty' which makes references to his own experiences in 1965 and 1969 while Adams was influenced by the film *Summer Of '42*.

'Summer Of '69' is a very nostalgic song built around the cultural revolution of the decade. Adams and Vallance had finished writing the song in the latter's basement in January 1984 but it went through a massive evolution as many songs often do. Ironically, at the time, neither of them thought it was a strong enough song for the album. The original demo was a twelve strong riff before it was replaced with a heavy six string sound. The duo recorded the song a few times before settling on the finished version. It was recorded about three or four times in its entirety, including demos, before they settled on the finished version. However, despite what we have come to believe, the song is not about the year but rather growing up, making love and looking fondly back at it.

Adams spoke to *The Celebrity Café*'s Dominick A. Miserandino in 2008 about the song: "We could take the cookie cutter out and we'd be slapping them out all the time. I think 'Summer Of '69' – I think it's timeless because it's about making love in the summertime. There is a slight misconception it's about a year, but it's not. '69' has nothing to do about a year, it has to do with a sexual position".

Recording took place at Little Mountain Sound Studios in Vancouver and was mixed in New York by Clearmountain with engineers Michael Sauvage and the esteemed Mike Fraser.

The album was finished by the end of November.

The recordings featured musicians Keith Scott on lead guitars, rhythm guitars and backing vocals, Jim Vallance on percussion, Dave Taylor on bass guitar, Pat Steward on drums and backing vocals, keyboardist Tommy Mandel, Jody Perpick on backing vocals and background sounds and Mickey Curry on drums with Tina Turner on lead vocals on the excellent 'It's Only Love'.

Jon Bon Jovi who had yet to make the big time with 1986's *Slippery When Wet* was impressed by Adams' songwriting as he told VH-1 in 2002: "I liked "I liked what Bryan Adams was doing with Tina Turner. So I asked our A&R guy, 'Can't I write a song for a Tina Turner and sing it with her?' He said: 'It's the publisher's job to get those songs out there, and your publisher's obviously not doing that. I know a guy who has lost his record deal and is hustling songs around. If you guys write with him, perhaps something good will come of it'. We thought: 'Why not? We'll see what happens'".

The track 'Heaven' was inspired by the Journey song 'Faithfully'. Adams had supported Journey on a hundred dates throughout 1983 on their *Frontiers* Tour during which time Adams and Vallance wrote 'Heaven' and recorded it at The Power Station in New York on June 6 and 7 1983. Drummer Mickey Curry had pre-warned Adams that he was on limited time and had to leave the sessions to continue his committed to a Hall &

Oates session. 'Heaven' was behind schedule and as such Adams called Steve Smith who was in NYC at the time to fill the vacant drumming position. Adams initially thought 'Heaven' was too lightweight for the album but he had a change of mind at the last minute and included it on the final tracklisting. The song initially appeared on the 1983 soundtrack to the movie *A Night In Heaven*. It was Adams and Vallance's first foray into movie soundtracks.

The film and its soundtrack were released in November 1983 and though the song made it into the Top 10 Mainstream Rock Chart in early 1984 Adams chose to release it as a single when the album came out.

Adams spoke to Deborah Wagner of *PopEntertainment* in 2005 about his fondness for ballads: "There was never a shift in direction. If you listen to my albums, they all rock and there are the occasional slow numbers. My first hit was 'Straight From The Heart' and my first number one was 'Heaven'. I've always done them".

Reckless peaked at Number 1 in the US *Billboard* charts in 1984. It contains the hit singles 'Run To You', 'Summer Of '69', 'Heaven', 'One Night Love Affair' and 'Somebody' as well as the Tina Turner duet 'It's Only Love'. 'Run To You', 'Summer Of '69' and 'Heaven' made the Top 10 in the US.

'Run To You' was the album's most successful single by far; it peaked at Number 1 and received heavy airplay while 'It's Only Love' was nominated for a Grammy Award for 'Best Rock Vocal Performance By A Duo Or Group'. The song later won an MTV Award for 'Best Stage Performance'.

Each single had an accompanying music video and helped make Adams a well-known figure in the music industry. The album's six singles made the US Top 15, a feat that had only been accomplished at the time by Michael Jackson's *Thriller* and Bruce Springsteen's *Born In The U.S.A.*

The Village Voice's Robert Christgau wrote in his famed *Consumer Guide*: "The megabuck stops here. Maybe I'll let Bruce Springsteen teach me how to hear John Cougar Mellencamp, but damned if I'm going to let John Cougar Mellencamp teach me how to hear Bryan Adams. From antipunkdiscowave strut to *Flashdance* homage, he's a generic American hunk, only whiter because he's Canadian. Where Sammy Hagar flaunts his anticommunism and Don Henley flaunts his mouth, Adams flaunts nothing more and nothing less than his young reliable bod. Like all the above-mentioned good and bad he shares a mysterious nostalgia for the recent past with a lot of people who aren't half dead yet, at least chronologically".

Christgau continued: "And more than any of them he has real problems relaxing, which puts him square in the soul-as-will-and-idea tradition of Lou Gramm, Pat Boone, Sophie Tucker, and so many others".

Rolling Stone's Christopher Connelly wrote: "For the gravel-on-velvet fans, *Reckless* does supply a fine slow song, 'Heaven', but that was a hit last year from a movie soundtrack. Ah, well – at this writing, *Reckless* is the most frequently played LP on album radio, and with its beautiful by-the-numbers sound, it's no wonder. Looking for challenge, adventure, excitement? Join the navy".

Reckless kicks off with the terrific rock ballad 'One Night Love Affair' before the deliciously melodic 'She's Only Happy When She's Dancin'' raises a smile. 'Run To You' is one of Adams' most iconic songs. A truly superb piece of music and a timeless rock song. 'Heaven' is one of Adams' greatest achievements as far as ballads go; it's a move, delicate piece of musicianship. 'Somebody' picks up the speed as the opening riff begins; it's an infectious slice of mid '80s Bryan Adams. 'Summer Of '69' is an all-time classic and a heavy fan favourite; played at parties, weddings and pubs all around the world, it's not lost any of its appeal over time. While some of Adams' ballads may have proved too twee for a majority of the 1980s rock crowd with 'Kids Wanna Rock' he proved that he had every intention of rockin' out. It's another classic song. 'It's Only Love' is one of the all-time great duets in rock music – the young, rising rock star paired with a living legend whose career was recently resurrected in remarkable style. The lead riff, vocals, lyrics and melody are in pristine condition. 'Long Gone' is another infectious rock song with a robust lead riff while the final song, 'Ain't Gonna Cry', is a fast-paced sing-it-out-loud rock number and closes the album perfectly.

Reckless is perhaps Adams' finest rock album and one of the greatest albums of its kind. With this album he proved that he could sing rock songs just as effectively as he could ballads.

Reckless helped Adams gain a nomination for 'Best Male Rock Performance' at the MTV Awards and it became Adams' best-selling album in the US and was certified Platinum five times. It sold over five million copies in the US alone and was the first Canadian album to sell over one million copies in Canada.

Around this time songs by Adams and Vallance began to appear elsewhere. 'Can't Wait All Night' from the same titled Julie Newton album in June 1984 was released as a single. The Krokus album *The Blitz*, released in August 1984, featured 'Boys Nite Out' co-credited to bandmembers Marc Storace and Fernando Von Arb. September 1984 saw the release of the film *Teachers*; its soundtrack featured two songs by Adams and Vallance: 'Teacher, Teacher' which was a Top 40 hit for .38 Special and 'Edge Of A Dream' which was a single by Joe Cocker.

The next two to three years was a whirlwind of activity with his touring band consisting of guitarist Keith Scott, bassist Dave Taylor, keyboarder Johnny "Blitz" Hannah and drummer Pat Steward.

Adams launched an enormous two year tour in December 1984 which commenced in the US with dates in Chicago, Detroit, New York City and Philadelphia with further US shows in early '85 and visits to Japan, Australia and the UK before finally flying back home to Canada. Further shows were added on the US West Coast finishing with two nights at the LA Palladium. During this time he won four Juno Awards.

Following the US tour he took part in the Canadian artists ensemble Northern Lights who recorded the song 'Tears Are Not Enough' (written by Adams with Vallance and David Foster) for the African famine relief effort which was no doubt in response to the British organized African charity Live Aid (with the single 'Do They Know It's Christmas') and subsequently USA For Africa (with 'We Are The World'). Adams hit the road again in April 1985 for a fifty date tour of Europe with singer Tina Turner.

Adams spoke to *Song Facts'* Carl Wiser in 2009 about working with Turner: "I used to go to see her in the clubs when I was in my late teens/early 20s before she hit the big time. It was incredible to watch her".

Adams continued: "Amazingly when we toured together years later, I never saw Tina walk through a performance, she always put on a great show, and was gracious and grateful to her audience. It was such a privilege to have sung with her, especially since I was only 24 at the time".

The tour ended with three sold out headlining shows of his own at the Hammersmith Odeon in London. Adams played his first high profile charity performance at the US Live Aid convert at JFK Stadium in Philadelphia. His twelve minute set consisted of 'Kids Wanna Rock', 'Summer Of '69', 'Tears Are Not Enough' and 'Cuts Like A Knife'.

"Things changing by the second..." he told Deborah Wagner of *PopEntertainment* in 2005 about the event. "I was introduced by Jack Nicholson in Philly in 1985; in fact he was the one that introduced me to the world! Thanks, Jack. I was just thinking that both stadiums that held the Live Aid concerts twenty years ago have been torn down, and it could have been the defining moment for both places".

If that tour wasn't enough Adams launched the World Wide In '85 Tour in Oklahoma and finished it in October. He also played shows in Vancouver and New York at the end of the year.

In August 1985 Loverboy included another Adams/Vallance track, 'Dangerous', on the *Lovin' Every Minute* album. It was released as a single and made the Hot 100.

1985 also saw Adams collaborate with The Who's Roger Daltrey on his sixth solo album *Under A Raging Moon*, which was billed as a tribute to The Who's drummer Keith Moon who died in 1978.

Adams co-wrote two tracks on the album with Vallance: 'Let Me Down Easy' and 'Rebel', which was reworked for Adams' next album. The former was a Top 15 hit on the *Billboard* Mainstream Rock Tracks chart and featured Adams on guitar and backing vocals next to Daltrey and guitarist Robbie McIntosh in the music video.

Adams cropped on as a guest vocalist on the Canadian band Glass Tiger's single 'Don't Forget Me (When I'm Gone)' which was produced by Vallance. The single was released in Canada in February 1986 and hit Number 1; eight months later it was released in the US and peaked at Number 2.

Further collaborations happened when in April 1986 Adams and Vallance's song 'No Way To Treat A Lady' was included on the Bonnie Tyler album *Secret Dreams*. As already mentioned Tyler had covered 'Straight From The Heart' on the mega-successful opus *Faster Than The Speed Of Night* and 'No Way To Treat A Lady' was also sung by Bonnie Raitt on the *Nine Lives* album.

The Adams and Vallance penned track 'It Should Have Been Me' was included on Neil Diamond's album, *Headed For The Future* which was released in May 1986.

With Adams as producer, 'It Should Have Been Me' was also included later in the year on the Carly Simon opus, *Coming Around Again*.

The Canadian duo of Adams and Vallance also contributed to 'Back Where You Started' on the Tina Turner album *Break Every Rule*, the lesser successful follow-up to her comeback album *Private Dancer*.

For such a young guy Adams was already very successful and in demand as both a singer and a songwriter. He had an incredible knack for penning popular songs with indelible lyrics, catchy melodies and neat riffs. He was now a global star with a couple of successful albums to his name and a stream of hit singles.

There was no stopping him now. The 1980s was his decade.

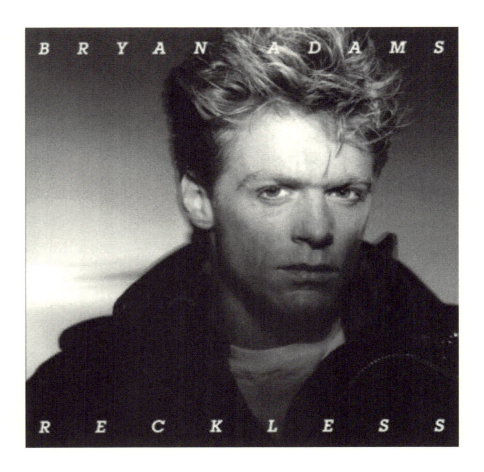

A CASUAL GUIDE TO THE MUSIC OF BRYAN ADAMS

INTO THE FIRE

"In fact, having a thick skin is important because very few people will give two shits about someone with weird hair and dodgy dress sense looking for a record deal"

- Speaking to Hester Lacey, *FT Magazine*, 2013

Adams followed the hugely successful *Reckless* with *Into The Fire*, released in 1987.

Into The Fire was recorded between mid-August and late October 1986 at a makeshift studio set up in Adams house with his backing band Keith Scott, Mickey Curry, Dave Taylor and Tommy Mandel. His house was nicknamed Cliffhanger because it was close to the sea in West Vancouver. They used various locations in the house, such as the dining room, bathroom and bedroom, to isolate the instruments to create different sounds. Most of the songs were written specifically for the album, though 'Hearts On Fire' was written in 1984 for *Reckless* but not recorded until September 1986 and later mixed in London, England.

Adams wanted a strong lyrical approach to the album having been inspired by the likes of U2, The Police and Peter Gabriel. Adams had been involved with those artists on the six date tour in 1986, Amnesty International Conspiracy Of Hope. Adams and Vallance were only contend with 'Victim Of Love' and 'Hearts On Fire' as they represented the approach Adams was now striving to take with his songwriting. The title of the album refers to a man at the crossroads of life which was how he felt at the time. The recordings were mixed at AIR Studios in London and Warehouse Studio in Vancouver.

It was a Top 10 hit in both the US and UK and features six singles 'Heat Of The Night', 'Hearts On Fire', 'Victim Of Love', 'Only The Strong Survive', 'Into The Fire' and 'Another Day'. The former two releases were moderately successful though 'Heat Of The Night;' charted in the UK.

"Let's face it, this business is built around songs and songs alone", he'd admitted to Gary James of *Classic Bands* back in 1982, and he's not wrong. "Radio stations would not play music unless they had good material, record companies would not be in business unless they had good songs. Artists would not be signing, unless there were good songs to sing. A lot of record companies get confused and they figure oh, we got to have a good looking band with lots of equipment and the singer has to have big, rosy lips. Wrong. It starts with songs first".

Though it sold two million copies worldwide it was somewhat disappointing in the aftermath of the enormous success of *Reckless*. The cover photograph of Adams were shot by the revered Dutch photographer Anton Corbijn at an unknown location.

Steve Hochman wrote in *Rolling Stone*: "...relying on crowd pleasers isn't enough for Adams anymore, and *Into The Fire* makes no case that he can grow beyond that. It's still possible that he has a Scarecrow in him – he's only twenty-seven, after all. But at this point he would appear to be stuck between his rock and a hard place".

Robert Christgau wrote: "...while 'Only The Strong Survive', the biggest offender with twelve, streamrollers across despite it all, neither Don Henley soul nor emergent social conscience justify the dumbness density. I know the salt of the earth is the shape of things to come, but these words of wisdom are beyond the pale".

Into The Fire opens with the excellent 'Heat Of The Night', which remains an absolute gem of his song, very understated and underrated. Adams gives it his all during 'Into The Fire' which has a distinctive bass line and chorus. 'Victim Of Love' is a fairly average ballad; there's nothing special about it but it fits well with the rest of the album. 'Another Day' is a fast rock with nifty some piano work and an effective mid-song guitar solo. 'Native Son' is an almost softly spoken ballad that would not seem out of place on a Sting album but at the same time there's something emotional and delicate about it. 'Only The Strong Survive' moves the album back into rock territory while 'Rebel' is another song that owes a debt of sorts to Bruce Springsteen. 'Remembrance Day' is a somewhat dated mid-paced rock ballad while 'Hearts On Fire' is one of the album's better tracks and another underrated gem. The final song, 'Home Again', is a moving mid-paced ballad with a terrific vocal performance.

Into The Fire sounds a little dated in the 2010s but at the same time it is perhaps his most underrated and underappreciated album. There are some truly great tracks on this album but sadly, it remains rather obscure.

Adams commenced the *Into The Fire* Tour in May 1987 with a show in Shreveport, Louisiana before heading to the UK for a performance at the Prince's Trust charity concert in Wembley Stadium in London. Shows continued in the US including two nights at Madison Square Garden in NYC where Adams would be visited by Brian Wilson of the Beach Boys. He stayed on the road to tour North American before heading back to the UK in October which included four consecutive sold out nights at Wembley Arena and further shows around Europe, including Ireland, and then it was on to a tour of Asia with five shows at the Budokan in Tokyo by which time *Into The Fire* had sold 100,000 copies in Japan and was certified Platinum.

The tour finished back in Europe where he played East and West Berlin before the tour's final night in Locarno, Switzerland. In totally, he was on the road from May 1987 to July 1988. One of the final shows, in Werchter, Belgium, was filmed for a television special called *Bryan Adams: Live In Belgium* which aired on Canadian TV on January 15, 1989.

Adams and Vallance continued to write songs for other artists: 'Back To Paradise' co-written with Pat Benatar was performed by .38 Special and used in the film *Revenge Of The Nerds II* in the summer of 1987. It was also released as a single. In August 'Hometown Hero' written with Adams was included on Loverboy's *Wildside* album.

1988 saw the release of the first ever Bryan Adams compilation, *Hits On Fire*, which was only issued in Japan. It's a two CD set: the first disc features the whole of the *Into The Fire* album while the second disc features singles from both *Cuts Like A Knife* and *Reckless* as well as songs that had not been released on CD outside of Japan and were included on the original 12" singles.

1989 saw the release of songs written by Adams and Vallance released by other artists and further collaborations. As soon as the *Into The Fire* Tour came to an end Adams involved himself in the Clint Eastwood film *Pink Cadillac*, which was released in the summer of 1989. Adams took a small part in the film and with Vallance co-wrote 'Drive All Night' which was sung by Dion.

Adams did some backing vocals on the *Dr. Feelgood* album by Mötley Crüe and also on 'Whatever It Takes' by Belinda Carlisle from her album, *Runaway Horses*.

Of the Crüe sessions he said to *Washingtonian*'s Sophie Gilbert: "Super fun. On a session one day there was Steve Tyler, me, the singer from Mötley Crüe. It was a giggle".

Adams, Vallance and Diane Warren wrote 'When The Night Comes' which was included on the Joe Cocker album *One Night Of Sin*, released in August 1989. It was issued as a single and made the Top 20. It became one of Adams and Vallance's last collaborations together for years.

They broke up their partnership in August 1989.

December 1989 saw the release of *Live! Live! Live!*, but only in Japan; a stronghold for Western rock bands. It was released elsewhere in the mid-1990s. To promote the release Adams played two New Year's shows in Japan.

Live! Live! Live! is a fine representation of what Adams was like onstage in the late 1980s. Of course, he is now the perfect stageman and his band are much tauter which comes with age and experience but *Live! Live! Live!* hits the spot. It features a suitable blend of songs from the ballads to the rockers, from the hits to the semi-obscure, including some covers: 'She's Happy When She's Dancin'', 'It's Only Love', 'Cut's Like A Knife', 'Kids Wanna Rock', 'Hearts On Fire', ' Take Me Back', 'The Best Was Yet To Come', 'Heaven', 'Heat Of The Night', ' Run To You', 'One Night Love Affair', 'Long Gone', 'Summer Of '69', 'Somebody', 'Walkin' After Midnight', 'I Fought The Law' and 'Into The Fire'.

On July 21 1990 Adams took part in *The Wall – Live In Berlin*, a concert by Roger Waters of Pink Floyd. The show featured an array of guests and celebrated the fall of the Berlin Wall; eight months earlier. Adams sang 'Empty Spaces' / 'What Shall We Do Now?' with Roger Waters and the Rundfunk Orchestra and Choir and 'Young Lust' with guitar solos by Rick Di Fonzo and Snowy White.

Much of the year was spent working on new material for his next album.

A CASUAL GUIDE TO THE MUSIC OF BRYAN ADAMS

WAKING UP THE NEIGHBOURS

"A songwriter writes songs all the time, whereas just writing a song can be done by anyone, anytime".

- Speaking to Alison Richter, *Examiner*, 2012

Bryan Adams' next album, *Waking Up The Neighbours*, was recorded at Battery Studios in London and at The Warehouse Studios in Vancouver, Canada between March 1990 and June 1991. Afterwards it was mixed at Mayfair Studios in London and mastered by Bob Ludwig at Masterdisk in NYC. The album was co-produced by Adams and Mutt Lange who is best known for producing the classic AC/DC albums *Highway To Hell* and *Back In Black* as well as his stellar work with Def Leppard and Foreigner.

Vallance had little input during the recording of the album though he did co-write some of the songs. 'There Will Never Be Another Tonight' was written in the late eighties as a sort of tribute to Buddy Holly with 'Peggy Sue' in mind. The demo was worked on by Adams and Lange.

Adams learned as much about writing songs and making music with Lange as he'd done with Vallance back in the 1980s. They also became good friends. Lange is a terrific musician and singer with a notable background producing rock albums. His way of making songs was markedly different from Vallance's. Lange would merge together two or three ideas from different songs into one song and that would trigger something in Adams who would contribute a title which would then spark the pair off into a riff. Adams learned not to be too obsessive over an idea and that it can change and you can be flexible with it.

The album features musicians Keith Scott (lead guitar), Tommy Mandel (keyboards/organ), Dave Taylor (bass), Mickey Curry (drums), Phil Nicholas (keyboards and programming), Robbie King (Hammond organ), Bill Payne (piano and Hammond organ), Larry Klein (bass), Ed Shearmur (keyboards) and The Tuck Back Twins (background vocals).

Waking Up The Neighbours is Adams' most successful and perhaps best known album to date. It peaked at Number 6 in the US but Number 1 in the UK and Germany in September 1991. It features the hugely successful single '(Everything I Do) I Do It For You', his second US Number 1 single. The song spent sixteen consecutive weeks at Number 1 in the UK singles charts (breaking a record previously held by Slim Whitman and Rose Marie in 1956) and also hit Number 1in France, Germany and Australia.

It featured in the blockbuster Hollywood movie *Robin Hood: Prince Of Thieves* starring Kevin Costner and Alan Rickman. He won a Grammy Award in 1991 for 'Best Song Written Specifically For A Motion Picture Or For Television'. The song was covered by R&B star Brandy in 1999.

Adams was approached by the producers of the album about working on a theme song.

He was handed a tape with orchestration of it written by composer Michael Kamen. Adams and Lange used the orchestration for the basis of '(Everything I Do) I Do It For You'; some of the orchestration as used in the final song.

Adams speaking to *Songwriter Universe's* Dale Kawashima: "Writing 'Everything I Do' with Mutt took about 45 minutes and it was a moment that I've only felt a few times – it's the moment when you know it's a good song, you don't know if it's a hit, you just know it's good. The track originally started from a long piece of orchestration written by film composer Michael Kamen (who I went on to write many more songs with) and we narrowed the theme down to the little piano intro at the beginning, and then we started writing a top line to it. Next time you check it out, notice the use of counter melodies, where the piano plays one thing and the vocal does another".

The single eventually sold ten million copies worldwide, more than any single since 'We Are The World'.

"How could it be an albatross?" he said to *The Guardian*'s Simon Hattenstone in 2002. "It's a moving piece of music and it's international. Everybody around the world got that song".

The album spawned several hit singles, including 'Can't Stop This Thing We Started' which peaked at Number 2 in the US and 'Do I Have To Say The Words?' which hit Number 11.

'Thought I Died And Gone To Heaven' was a chart hit in the UK. 'There Will Never Been Another Tonight', 'All I Want Is You' and 'Touch The Hand' were also issued as singles and have music videos to accompany them. As a side note the music video for 'There Will Never Been Another Tonight' was filmed at Sheffield Arena and actress Rachel Weisz can be seen in the audience.

Waking Up The Neighbors was his most successful album since *Reckless*, selling four million copies in the US alone and another six million around the world and hitting Number 1 in seventeen countries. The album earned six Grammy nominations and a Grammy nomination the following year for 'Best Rock Male Vocalist' for 'There Will Never Be Another Tonight'.

Gina Arnold wrote in *Entertainment Weekly*: "Adams' first studio LP in four years, the incredibly tuneful *Waking Up The Neighbours*, uses every surefire hit-single formula known to mankind, but it's so smooth it lacks all personality. And, except on his recent big hit, Adams is startlingly unromantic. He has all the soul of a sentimental green cheese".

Rolling Stone's James Hunter wrote: "*Waking Up The Neighbours'* will, with no sweat, reestablish Bryan Adams as the radio's hoarse purveyor of energy and fun… Like most capable pop craftsmen hellbent on seizing the airwaves, Adams and Lange walk a fine line between familiarity and derivativeness, between the blazingly immediate and the outright stale. So some tunes on *Waking Up The Neighbours* have turned out too broad for anyone's taste".

The album was also in the press not only because of its enormous success but because Lange was of British-Zambian descent and because the album was not entirely recorded in Canada under the rules at the time it meant that the album did not qualify as Canadian. Adams voiced his complaints about the rules and in September 1991 the Canadian Radio-Television and Telecommunications Commission (CRTYC) broadened the rules allowing freer collaborations between Canadians and non-Canadians.

"You know what I really would like to do", Adams confessed to Simon Hattenstone of *The Guardian* in 2002. "I always just wanted to be the singer or the bass player in the band. I'd love to have a band, where I was obviously the singer, but where it wasn't me, it wasn't my name. That's why you never see anything about me. I've never been enamoured by the idea of being a celebrity. When 'Everything I Do' was number one for four months, I don't think I did one interview. All I wanted to do was have a band".

Waking Up The Neighbours opens with the cheeky rocker 'Is Your Mama Gonna Miss Ya?' before the equally boisterous 'Hey Honey – I'm

Packin' You In!' kicks into action. Adams sounds like he's having a blast so far. 'Can't Stop This Thing We Started' remains a live fixture in his setlists and one of his most infectious songs. It's an absolute classic.

'Thought I'd Died And Gone To Heaven' is a fairly sombre ballad but all the more moving while 'Not Guilty' is an understated rockin' gem of a song. 'Vanishing' shifts the album up a notch and is an effective little number while 'House Arrest' is toe-tapping fun. 'Do I Have To Say The Words?' slows the album down but it's a moving ballad that borders on twee but is saved by a terrific vocal performance. 'There Will Never Be Another Tonight' and 'All I Want Is You' solid rock songs with finely-crafted melodies. 'Depend On Me' is a well-played mid-paced ballad with a sturdy lead riff. '(Everything I Do) I Do It For You' needs no description whatsoever. It has become THAT song in Adams' cannon. 'If You Wanna Leave Me (Can I Come Too?)' is a rock steady track with some excellent keys and vocals. 'Touch The Hand' opens with strong lead riff that is maintained throughout the song and the closing number 'Don't Drop That Bomb On Me' is a five minute Def Leppard style over-produced anthemic rocker.

Waking Up The Neighbours has gone Mutt Lange's signature all over it and Bryan Adams is all the better for it. He's never sounded this good as a singer and guitarist. As far as a rock sound goes, this is his strongest album. Hands down.

Adams had already been on the road when the album was released having co-headlined shows in Europe with Texan blues boogie masters ZZ Top beginning June 8.

To promote the album Adams launched the Waking Up The World Tour in October 1991 in Belfast, Northern Ireland and ran to May 1993. The tour included many key events, including two shows in Reykjavik, Iceland and a show at the Ritz in NYC which sold out in less than two hours and featured Ben E. King and Nona Hendryx in attendance. The Canadian leg of the world tour commenced on January 13 1992 and finished on the thirty-first with a standing room only gig in Vancouver. In February he played shows in New Zealand and Australia before heading to Japan and then onto the UK and Europe in the summer. He performed for the first time ever in Hungary and Turkey where he filmed the video for 'Do I Have To Say The Words?' with director Anton Corbijn. The concert, filmed at BJK İnönü Stadiumon June 28, 1992, was the first outdoor stadium show in Istanbul history with 20,000 fans attending.

From September to December 1992 the tour travelled around the US before an Asian leg featuring Thailand, Singapore, Japan and Hong Kong in February 1992 before flying back to the US for a leg from March to May culminating in his final shows.

The tour featured a gig at Green Point stadium in Cape Town in South Africa after the release of Nelson Mandela and other political prisoners but it has so far been left undocumented, though concerts during apartheid times played by such artists as Queen and Paul Simon's collaborations with black South Africans on his hugely successful *Graceland* album have been heavily written about and much criticised. Adams' shows were sponsored by Coca-Cola and featured a commercial to promote the event. Adams and his band feature in the commercial played the song 'House Arrest'. Actress Neve Campbell was also in the commercial.

A compilation called *So Far So Good* was released in November 1993 and topped the album charts in various countries such as the UK, Germany and Australia. The collection included a brand new song called 'Please Forgive Me' which was a Number 1 hit in Australia and reached the Top 5 in the US, UK and Germany. The collection includes hit songs from *Cuts Like A Knife* (1983) to *Waking Up The Neighbors* (1991). 'Kids Wanna Rock' a popular live song and a fixture in his setlists, is the only track on the collection not to have been released as a single, though a number of live recordings had made appearances on various B-sides from 1984 to 1992. It's by no means the definitive collection as it misses some vital songs, notably, 'Hearts On Fire', 'Thought I'd Died And Gone To Heaven' and 'Victim Of Love'.

Adams was going to include the new song 'So Far So Good' as the first track so it would start and end with new songs but the idea was dropped in favour of opening with 'Summer Of '69' and closing with the new track 'Please Forgive Me'. 'So Far So Good' was later included on the two CD set *Anthology*.

'So Far So Good' was written in France in 1993 with a whole band in the studio. Adams had never worked with some of the musicians before such as piano player David Paich. They had recorded *Waking Up The Neighbours* instrument by instrument rather than with a full band unit so it made a refreshing change for Adams.

As is often the case with collections of this sort there have been various reissues and repackages since its original release with the inclusion of 'All For Love' and 'Have You Ever Really Loved A Woman?'. *So Far So Good* has sold over ten million copies since its original release.

Sputnikmusic's Mark Stebbing later enthused: "Adams is a likeable rebel, a tough and tender troubadour singing songs that may not have been taken seriously by rock critics, but which nevertheless had resonance for millions of people around the world. Between ballads like 'Heaven' and '(Everything I Do) I Do It For You' and the chest-thumping frat-guy rock of 'Somebody', this set shows the immense range of one of Canada's most popular musicians".

Dimitri Ehrlich of *Entertainment Weekly* wrote: "Adams never claimed he was born to be wild, but his rich chromatic choruses and epic productions were born to be broadcast on FM radio. Inoffensive on a colossal scale".

Other songs written by Adams appeared elsewhere such as 'Feels Like Forever', co-written with Diane Warren which appeared on the Joe Cocker album *Night Falls* in July 1992. 'Why Must We Wait Until Tonight?' written by Adams and Mutt Lange was sung and released as a single by Tina Turner. It appeared on the soundtrack to the movie of her life, *What's Love Got To Do With It?*.

In 1993 he hooked up with Rod Stewart and Sting for the hit single 'All For Love' (co-written with Lange and Michael Kamen) penned for the Disney movie *Three Musketeers*. It was a massive hit reaching Number 1 around the world. It hit Number 1 in the US on January 22, 1994. He also launched a tour of the Far East in January including such places as Vietnam, rarely visited by western pop artists.

Adams released his first live album *Live! Live! Live!* in 1994. The recordings actually took place back in 1988 at the Rock Werchter Festival in Belgium on July 3 except for 'Into The Fire' which was recorded in Tokyo. It sold over a million copies.

Chuck Eddy wrote in *Entertainment Weekly*: "*Live! Live! Live!*, (culled from two shows) wisely focuses on riff-stomping shout-alongs. His stage patter is comically bland ('Here's another song you might know'), but he barks his hits robustly and covers 'I Fought The Law' with outlaw urgency".

Mostly, though, his profile was relatively low in 1994 and early 1995 as he began work on a new album.

Adams came back into the limelight and released a single in 1995 called 'Have You Ever Really Loved A Woman?' (co-written with Lange and Kamen) from the Johnny Depp/Marlon Brando movie *Don Juan DeMarco*. The song hit Number 1 in the US and Australia and was a Top 5 success in the UK and Germany. It was nominated for a Grammy for 'Best Male Pop Vocal Performance' and an Oscar nomination for 'Best Song'. In late 1995 he collaborated with Bonnie Raitt on 'Rock Steady' (co-penned with Gretchen Peters) on her live album *Road Tested*. It was released as a single.

What would the rest of the decade bring for Bryan Adams?

A CASUAL GUIDE TO THE MUSIC OF BRYAN ADAMS

18 TIL I DIE

"I keep touring. I've always done a lot of shows. I reckon I probably do 100 to 120 shows a year and it's been like that since I can remember. Back in the '90s it would have been more – it would have been close to 200 shows a year".

- Speaking to Nathan Woods, *MaxTV*, 2012

There was no rush to follow *Waking Up The Neighbours* because it had been so successful so Adams could take his time crafting new material. However, the success of *Waking Up The Neighbours* also meant that Adams' next album would be surround by a great deal of hype.

Adams returned to the studio for *18 Til I Die*. It was the first album not to include any songs by long-time collaborator Jim Vallance and was written, recorded and produced by Adams and Mutt Lane at a house in Ocho Rios, Jamaica from late 1994 to the summer of 1995 and further work was completed at two separate houses in Provence, France from late 1995 to early 1996. The pair used The Warehouse Studio Mobile Unit. Curiously, the album was also mixed in Provence by Bob Clearmountain.

The album features Keith Scott on lead guitar, flamenco guitarist Paco de Lucia on 'Have You Ever Really Loved A Woman?', drummer

Mickey Curry, Dave Taylor on bass, Olle Romo on percussion, Michael Kamen on piano and string arrangements and Mutt Lange on guitars.

Adams and Lange had a dozen songs completed by 1995 but went back to the studio to record two more songs as they felt the album was missing something. They subsequently crafted 'The Only Thing That Looks Good On Me Is You' and '18 Til I Die'. He'd already begun playing some tracks onstage before the album's release, including 'Let's Make A Night To Remember' which was played at a soundcheck for a 1993 gig on the *So Far So Good* World Tour.

The album, poorly received by critics, only made it to Number 31 in the US *Billboard* 200. It had far better successful Europe where it hit Number 1 in the UK and was a Top 10 hit in various European countries as well as Australia. It was certified Platinum in the US and three times Platinum in Canada and Australia and twice in the UK. It sold three million copies.

Edna Gundersen wrote in *USA Today*: "Many albums ago, Adams could lay claim to teen turf, but he's too grizzled and creatively stymied to pull off kid stuff like the comically adolescent '(I Wanna Be) Your Underwear'. Adams' serviceable pop vocals are better suited to his usual schmaltzy ballads and lite midlife rock".

"The blues-rocking 'Do To You' and tender 'I'll Always Be Right There' merit notice", Gundersen continued, "but the wimpy 'You're Still Beautiful To Me' and 1995's sap 'n' salsa show tune, 'Have You Ever Really Loved A Woman?', are enough to make you yawn".

David Browne wrote in *Entertainment Weekly*: "*18 Til I Die* is hackwork, yet hackwork so upfront about its intentions and so eager to please that it's hard to despise".

The album spawned the singles 'The Only Thing That Looks Good One Me', 'Let's Make A Night To Remember', 'I'll Always Be Right There', 'Star' and '18 Til I Die'. The former single undoubtedly became the album's most popular track reaching Number 4 in the UK, though 'Have You Ever Really Loved A Woman?' was a Number 1 hit on the US *Billboard* Hot 100.

Critics noted that the album is patchy with a lack of focus as the album shifts from blues to rock to ballads and they also claimed that the songwriting was below par as past Bryan Adams albums had been consistent.

18 Til I Die starts with the awesome guitar-laden 'The Only Thing That Looks Good On Me Is You', which has since became a fixture in his setlists. It's classic Bryan Adams. 'Do To You' is a catchy harmonic-induced little number.

'Let's Make A Night To Remember' is a fondly thought of ballad and one of his better slow numbers while the title track, '18 Til I Die', is an absolute joy. A joyous sing-along arena rock song. 'Star' is an overproduced slow ballad, though, curious it trues too hard. '(I Wanna Be) Your Underwear' is a cheeky rocker and doesn't deviant from a mid-paced feel; the mid-song guitar solo saves it. 'We're Gonna Win' doesn't quite work – the vocals and instruments seem unbalanced somehow and Adams' voice sounds strained. 'I Think About You' is a curious little ballad that is suited to his aging voice.

'I'll Always Be Right There' is an acoustic number with a strong chorus while 'It Ain't A Party…If You Can't Come 'Round' picks up speed after some slower numbers and the album kicks up a gear or two. It's a solid if distinctly average rock number. 'Black Pearl' has a gritty almost bluesy feel to it with references to Mississippi, which works while 'You're Still Beautiful To Me' is a dulcet ballad that hints at the sort of territory he would steer towards in later years. The closing song, 'Have You Ever Really Loved A Woman?', remains one of his best known songs and strongest ballads.

18 Til I Die is a curiosity. Overproduced in parts and desperate for attention, it has some killer tracks but the whole thing feels unbalanced. Still, it was his last truly memorable album as a whole.

He launched the eighteen month long *18 Til I Die* Tour of North America and Europe to promote the album. It kicked off in May 1996 in Tallinn, Estonia. On July 27 Adams played a show at London's Wembley Stadium in from of 70,000 fans; it was a sold out gig and is often considered to be his biggest ever headlining show. The show went live to twenty-five countries and was seen live by fans all over the world.

In 1996 Adams joined Eagles singer Don Henley onstage with a duet of 'Everybody Knows' at Live At Honors. In late 1996 Adams released another duet, this time with Barbra Streisand on 'I Finally Found Someone' which was co-written with Lange, Streisand and Marvin Hamlisch. It was the lead song for her movie *The Mirror Has Two Faces* and was a Top 10 hit and earned him a third Oscar nomination.

Adams had a hit single in June 1997 with 'You Walked In' written by Adams and Lange but performed by the country music band Lonestar and included on their *Crazy Nights* album. It was a Top 20 country hit and was also a Hot 100 hit. With Jean-Jacques Goldman and Eliot Kennedy Adams co-wrote 'Let's Talk About Love' which was the lead song for the Celine Dion album in November 1997. The album sold over ten million copies in the US alone.

In December 1997 Adams released *MTV Unplugged*, a live acoustic album. It was recorded in its entirety on September 26, 1997 at the Hammerstein Ballroom in NYC where he was accompanied by composer

Michael Kamen who brought students from the esteemed Juilliard School of Music to play with them. Irish piper Davy Spillane also joined Adams. The album features three brand new cuts: 'Back To You', 'A Little Love' and 'When You Love Someone'. 'If Ya Wanna Be Bad – Ya Gotta Be Good' was also performed and as such makes its first appearance on an album: it was originally a B-side to the 'Let's Make A Night To Remember' single. Adams also performed 'Hey Elvis' though it appears on neither the CD nor DVD, both of which have different tracklistings. The first single released from the album was the aforementioned 'Back To You' which was followed by 'I'm Ready' and an acoustic version of 'Cuts Like A Knife'.

MTV Unplugged was a Top 10 hit in Germany and sold over half a million copies worldwide. It was a stopgap between studio albums more than anything else.

Entertainment Weekly's Chuck Eddy wrote: "Adams omits a few of his more rocking hits in favour of schmaltz on *Unplugged*, but mostly he has fun taking chances on his acoustic gig".

Unplugged is a terrific release and one of the best in the series, even up there with Eric Clapton's hugely successful and revered *Unplugged* album. Adams has the audience in the palm of his hands and as the perfect showman he relishes every minute of it. His band are superlative, his voice is in terrific shape and the songs are finely constructed with an acoustic setting. Some of the sounds are really quite interesting, acoustically, and there's some fine arrangements and instrumentation. There's an even mix and tempos and the sound is nice and clear. He whisks through 'Summer Of '69', 'Back To You'', 'Cuts Like A Knife', 'I'm Ready', 'Fits Ya Good', 'When You Love Someone', '18 Til I Die', 'I Think About You', 'If Ya Wanna Be Bad – Ya Gotta Be Good', 'Let's Make A Night To Remember', 'The Only Thing That Looks Good On Me Is You', 'A Little Love', 'Heaven' and 'I'll Always Be Right There'.

Sadly, in terms of rock albums, *18 Til I Die* would be his last all-out rock effort.

ON A DAY LIKE TODAY

"I think my ethic today is probably as strong as ever. I don't think that has really changed. I think what has happened is there are a lot more places to play than ever before. I mean, hopefully I'm a better songwriter than I used to be".

- Speaking to John Newlin, *Zimbio*, 2012

After the unnecessary critical attacks on *18 Til I Die* Adams recruited esteemed producer Bob Rock best known for his work with such varied artists as Metallica, Aerosmith, Bon Jovi and Mötley Crüe to produce *On A Day Like Today*, which was recorded throughout 1997 and 1998. As with *18 Til I Die*, the album does not feature any songs written with Jim Vallance. The album features several songwriting partners but mostly Gretchen Peters.

After years working with Vallance and Lange, Adams had forged a new partnership. Adams is a great admirer of Gretchen Peters; her way with words is inspiring.

The recording sessions included Mickey Curry on drums, Keith Scott on bass and guitar, Phil Thornalley on guitar, bass and string arrangements, Dave Pickell on piano and organ and Danny Cummings on percussion. By side-lining ballads it was obvious that Adams was trying to re-establish himself as a rocker of the old days.

On A Day Like Today was released in 1998 and was Adams' first album since 1981's *You Want It, You Got It* not to be certified by the RIAA. A&M sold his recording contract to Interscope and the album, though, not a major success due in part to a reported lack of promotion especially in the States, fared well in Germany and the UK. The album also hit number three in Canada.

It had two Top 10 British singles with 'Cloud Number Nine' and 'When You're Gone' which was a duet with Mel C of the Spice Girls. The single sold 676,947 copies and was the eighty-second bestselling single of the 1990s and has become a fixture in his setlist; he picks out a female member of the audience to sing it with him.

Tom Lanham wrote of the album in *Entertainment Weekly*: "Like Clapton and Mellencamp before him, multiplatinum Canadian crooner Bryan Adams has started searching for that perfect balance of mature grace and useful guitar grind. No fumbling around during *On A Day Like Today*; Adams' new restraint energizes this gently jangling material".

One A Day Like Today starts off with the overly sentimental but oddly effective ballad 'How Do Ya Feel Tonight' while 'C'mon C'mon C'mon' is a slightly heavier number but still firmly rooted in the same sort of territory. 'Getaway' is perhaps the album's standout track with some neat production tricks. 'On A Day Like Today' is an acoustic based ballad while 'Fearless' kicks the album up a gear but the whole album feels far too twee and laidback. He continues his middle of the road journey with 'I'm A Liar' but 'Cloud Number Nine' is perhaps the album's better song at the same time being one of its most famous. At last a rock song is delivered with the terrific 'When You're Gone', a duet with Mel C. 'Inside Out' is a below C grade ballad and 'If I Had You' is a similar sort of whispery, slow love song. 'Before The Night Is Over' picks up some speed but only hints at the sort of rock ballad that Adams is famous far. Maybe he's showing his age but the album so far is very middle of the road and almost bland. Said track is a pretty decent mid-paced rocker.

'I Don't Wanna Live Forever' thankfully follows a similar sort of pattern – decent riff, drums and a catchy chorus. 'Where Angels Fear To Tread' slows proceedings down considerably as does the closing track 'Lie To Me'.

Despite two or three passable rock songs, *On A Day Like Today* has too many production effects and slow numbers. It's distinctly middle of the road and after the gritty riffs of *18 Til I Die* Adams moves away from the vibrant melodic rock that made his name. Good in parts, weak in others but overall a disappointment compared to his other albums.

Bryan White released a country version of 'You're Still Beautiful To Me', the Adams and Lange song which appeared on *18 Til I Die*.

White's 'You're Still Beautiful To Me' was released in June 1999 and made the country Top 40.

To celebrate his career and the millennium he released *The Best Of Me* featuring his most well-known songs. It includes two brand new songs: 'The Best Of Me' and 'Don't Give Up' which peaked at Number 1 in the UK. The US leg of A&M initially declined to release it. It was released in various packages, including a Special Tour Edition. The title-track was written with Mutt Lange making it their first collaboration since *18 Til I Die*. The collection was a Top 10 hit in Germany and was certified Platinum three times in Canada and once in the UK. The album was not a success in the US when it was finally issued in 2001 and neither were any of the singles hits. *The Best Of Me* is a decent mix of the old and new and while it isn't arguably the best of Bryan Adams it represents his most commercial songs. Some deep cuts would have add more depth. It is certainly a fantastic introduction for new fans.

Andy Orrell enthused on *Entertainment Scene 360*: "Overall this is a very good album. Some of the new songs are pretty average but the classics are all there. Adams has produced some class music over the last few decades and this is a really good reminder. If you are a fan of Bryan Adams, this is an album I'm sure you will really enjoy".

Much of the early 2000s was spent on various projects both in and out of the studio. He wrote a song (and sang) 'Don't Give Up' for the 2000

Chicane album *Behind The Sun*. Adams also appears in the video. He'd been absent from the US charts for over a year and 'Don't Give Up' also marked his appearance on the US dance charts in over two decades. It was a Number 3 dance hit in the spring of 2000.

In 2002 he wrote (with revered film composer Hans Zimmer) and played songs for the DreamWorks animated movie *Spirit: Stallion Of The Cimarron*. Working on the album made music exciting for Adams at the turn of the century. He was enthusiastic again and learned a great deal more about music from Zimmer.

"I wrote songs with a few different film composers, Hans Zimmer, the late Michael Kamen and even the late Marvin Hamlisch", he said to *Reverb Online*'s Courtney Laura. "As I said, I'm not bad at working with other people's scores and finding a way to make songs from them. Most of the songs happened from me being approached by them to collaborate".

The most successful song from the soundtrack was 'Here I Am' which was a Top 5 hit in the UK and Germany. He was also awarded a Golden Globe nomination for 'Best Song From A Motion Picture'.

Melodic.net's Kaj Roth enthused: "Bryan sings fantastic and full hearted, I must say I nearly gave up on him after *18 Til I Die* and *On A Day Like Today* which I wasn't too fond of....and then all these collections and unplugged things, it seemed his best days were over but how wrong I was! This is my first 5 rating since I started writing reviews on this site and

I thought I'd never hear a record that would make my knees weak again like this one did. We're talking classic albums like Rush-*Moving Pictures*, Journey – *Escape* and Vanhalen – s/t [self-title] to mention a few with 5 rating".

Opening with the surprisingly moving 'Here I Am', *Spirit: Stallion Of The Cimarron* is an effective collection of sixteen songs. 'I Will Always Return' is a powerful ballad while 'You Can't Take Me' has some powerful production effects and a strong melody. 'Get Off My Back' is a kick ass rocker and the album's standout track. 'Brothers Under The Sun' is an average ballad though there are some effective lyrics. 'Don't Let Go' is a duet with Sarah McLachlan and their voices really bounce well with each other. 'This Is Where I Belong' is a curious track with an African vibe and 'Here I Am' is a wishful number. 'Sound The Bugle' and 'Run Free' follow a similar journey with some fantastic instrumentation and ambience. 'Homeland' (Main Title) is a finely crafted instrumental piece as is 'Rain'. 'The Long Road Back' is a seven minute long instrumental that vividly evokes scenes from the animated film. 'Nothing I've Ever Known' is evocatively sung while Adams pours his heart into 'I Will Always Return (Finale)' and the closing number 'Where Do I Go From Here' is a typical modern day Bryan Adams ballad.

The album is an inspiring piece of work with some truly moving songs. A total surprise.

Also in 2002, a dance version of Adams and Vallance's 'Heaven' was recorded by DJ Sammy & Yanou Featuring DO and spent nine weeks at the top of the *Billboard* maxi singles chart.

Of course Adams toured extensively in support of his recent work. His show at Elysee Arena, Turku, Finland on February 12 2002 was reviewed by *Rock United*'s Kimmo Toivonen: "The whole show had a very intimate feeling, Bryan was in a good mood and joked and told little stories in-between the songs. It was more like a 'singalong get-together with Bryan' than a Big Rock Spectacle, and I wouldn't have traded it for one! As for the intimacy, Bryan took the idea of 'crowd participation' to another level by first handing out his microphone to the first row a couple of times, and then by inviting one girl to sing 'When You're Gone' with him. Paulina was probably the happiest girl in the arena".

2003 saw the release of the CD/DVD set *Live At The Budokan*, which was recorded at the famed Nippon Budokan Hall in Tokyo, Japan on June 15 and 16, 2000.

In 2004 he made the press after *ARC Weekly* released its top pop artist's chart of the last twenty-five years. Adams came in at Number 13 with four Number 1 singles, ten Top 5 singles and 17 Top 10 hits.

Adams isn't one to slow down and take a break. He had more work to complete in the studio and onstage.

A CASUAL GUIDE TO THE MUSIC OF BRYAN ADAMS

ROOM SERVICE

"Sometimes, but writing usually happens when I lock myself away in some foreign place – usually Paris – and I focus on getting all the ideas I've been collecting into songs".

- Speaking to Deborah Wagner, *PopEntertainment*, 2005

Room Service, his first full length album since *On A Day Like Today* and his first collection of recordings since the soundtrack album *Spirit: Stallion Of The Cimarron* in 2002, was released in September 2004. Adams produced the album and co-wrote the songs with Gretchen Peters, Nicholas Bracegirdle, Phil Thornalley, Robert John "Mutt" Lange, Eliot Kennedy and Jörgen Elofsson.

Adams had begun working on material that would become *Room Service* in 2001 at The Warehouse Studio in Vancouver but was interrupted by the *Spirit* soundtrack and a headlining tour of Europe. The Warehouse Studio is his own studio, which has been used by the likes of AC/DC over the years.

"You know, when I built the studio", he told Nathan Wood of *MaxTV* in 2012, "which was back in the early '90s, the idea was just that I wanted to have a place – because there wasn't anywhere decent to work. I always had to travel somewhere to go make records. We made some records in Vancouver, but then we'd always have to go to New York or somewhere to finish them up. I thought, 'Why do we have to do that? Let's just do something here'. So, I did that – [it was] very ambitious – a lot of people thought it was stupid. But, you know, it's kept its head above water, even in these difficult time, because people still want to make records. They still want to record. I'm actually very proud that it's had so many brilliant people come through there. I mean, everyone's been through there it seems".

He tried to make use of his free time on tour by working on overdubs and bits of recording as he'd become fed up and bored of working months at a time in the studio. Adams was able to get enough gear into some suitcases to create a makeshift studio in a couple of hotel rooms and order room service. Jackson Browne's *Running On Empty* was recording in a similar fashion.

For example, 'Open Road' was recorded across two continents while on tour – the basic recording was completed in Vancouver with vocals finished in Paris while guitarist Keith Scott completed his guitars in Lethbridge, Alberta over in Canada. Ben Dobie, Avril Mackintosh, and Olle Romo were on hand for some protocols editing.

Musicians featured on the album include Keith Scott (guitars), Mickey Curry (drums), Norm Fisher (bass), Gary Breit (piano and organ), Phil Thornalley (additional production, guitars and keyboards), Yoad Nevo (additional production, programming, percussion and guitars), Declan Masterson (Irish whistle on 'Flying'), Maurice Seezer (accordion and piano on 'Flying'), Gavin Greenway (string arrangement on 'Flying'), Michael Kamen (string arrangement and oboe on 'I Was Only Dreaming') and The Pointless Brothers (background vocals on 'Flying').

Though *Room Service* received mixed reviews from critics after its September 2004 release it peaked at Number 1 in Germany and Switzerland and Number 4 in the UK. It sold almost half a million copies in Europe during its first week of *release*. It debuted at Number 1 on the *Billboard* European album chart but was only released in May 2005 in the US without a record label and charted at Number 134 on the *Billboard* 200. The album sold three million copies.

Room Service spawned the successful single 'Open Road' which peaked at Number 1 in Canada and Number 21 in the UK. 'Flying', 'Room Service', 'This Side Of Paradise' and' Why Do You Have To Be So Hard To Love?' were also issued as singles.

Awarding the album only two stars out of ten Christ Jones wrote in *Uncut*: "Adams' instinctive grasp of classic rock idioms can sound as if he's doing it by numbers, while his ballads sometimes sound like a poor man's Rod Stewart. But despite its inherently conservative nature, *Room Service* is still a better record than you might imagine".

A CASUAL GUIDE TO THE MUSIC OF BRYAN ADAMS

Rolling Stone's David Wild wrote: "The songs are solidly constructed and catchy, and a few standouts, like 'EastSide Story' and 'This Side Of Paradise', display an emotional maturity that suits the guy far better than the aging horn-dog pose he struck back on 1996's *18 Til I Die*. For the faithful, at least, *Room Service* still delivers".

BBC.co.uk's Michelle Adamson wrote: "This album is classic Adams stuff and his fans will buy it in their legions. In fact, the distinctly country and western hue to *Room Service* will no doubt delight his American audience and guarantee heavy rotation on radio stations stateside. What is a reasonable start to the album quickly descends to an unforgiveable low point by track, 'Flying'".

Andrew McNeice wrote on *Melodicrock.com*: "A consistent and enjoyable album from Bryan that doesn't match his classic best, but is decent enough to please fans and suggest that the singer/songwriter still has a lot to offer. A little more guitar and a little more rock n roll might have spiced things up even further, but thank God the lame lyrics have been left behind".

Room Service opens with 'East Side Story' is a surprisingly vivid mid-paced ballad while 'This Side Of Paradise' follows a similar vibe. 'Not Romeo Not Juliet' is an effective number with an indelible chorus. 'Flying' and 'She's A Little Too Good For Me' are both consistent tracks with some effective songwriting. 'Open Road' is one of the album's more memorable songs with a riff that hints at vintage Bryan Adams. 'Room Service' is a toe-tapping song that works well on the live stage. 'I Was Only Dreamin'' is an average slow number even by Adams' standards. 'Right Back Where I Started From' is a pretty good contemporary melodic rock track with a sturdy lead riff and some expert musicianship. 'Nowhere Fast' and 'Why Do You Have To Be So Hard To Love' are both made of similar DNA while 'Blessing In Disguise' is the closing bonus track and it's a hoot.

Room Service has some good songs on offer and while it is a stronger album that *On A Day Like Today* it fails to match his finest work.

The *Room Service* Tour was very successful with mostly sold out shows from 2004 to 2006 vising such countries as India, Pakistan and Vietnam. Adams became the first Western artist to perform in Pakistan in 2006 at Karachi.

Adams released yet another compilation, this time the comprehensive two CD set *Anthology* which contained two new tracks.

The American version of the release featured a new version of 'When You're Gone' with Mel C. There's a good mix of classic driving rock, ballads and duets as well as his soundtrack singles. It's more comprehensive than *The Best Of Me* and appeals to both die-hard and casual Adams fans.

Some of the newer tracks fail to live up to what can be argued is vintage Adams circa 1983-1991. *Anthology* is an accurate example of his obvious talents.

Speaking to Dale Kawashima of *Songwriter Universe*: "The *Anthology* was the idea of Richie Gallo at the US record company, Universal. I ended up changing the selection of songs a few times to get something that wasn't just a hits package. It was an interesting project as it pushed me to dig up photos and technical notes from the '80s and '90s of when songs were written, recorded and mixed and so on – something for the fans that know these songs and would like more detail. Basically, it was a trip down memory lane".

The collection peaked at Number 65 on the *Billboard* 200 on its October 2005 release; Number 29 in the UK but Number 4 in Canada.

BlogCritics Julie wrote: "*Anthology* sums up the 25 year, multi-platinum career of a talented and unpretentious Canadian, who has forever framed the memories of our youth with his raspy voice and heart-felt songs. It will make a great stocking stuffer this Christmas".

In 2005 Adams also re-recorded the theme song for the second season of the Pamela Anderson sitcom *Stacked*. It was included on the US version of *Anthology*.

It didn't make sense to include the Mel C version and Adams wanted it to have a new angle so he called Anderson and she agreed to do it.

Adams released the entertaining *Live In Lisbon* in 2005 on DVD, though in the US it was released as the bonus disc on the two CD set, *Anthology*. The concert shows what an expert live performer he is as he runs through his hits and recent songs.

Adams' career in film flourish throughout the decade as 2005 also saw the release of the soundtrack EP, *Colour Me Kubrick*.

Moving in 2006 and Adams wrote and performed the theme song 'Never Let Go' for the Kevin Costner and Ashton Kutcher movie *The Guardian*. He also co-wrote the song 'Never Gonna Break My Faith' for the film *Bobby*. The song was later performed by Aretha Franklin and Mary J. Blige. Adams was awarded with a Golden Globe nomination in 2007 for the song. He was finally getting the recognition that he deserved.

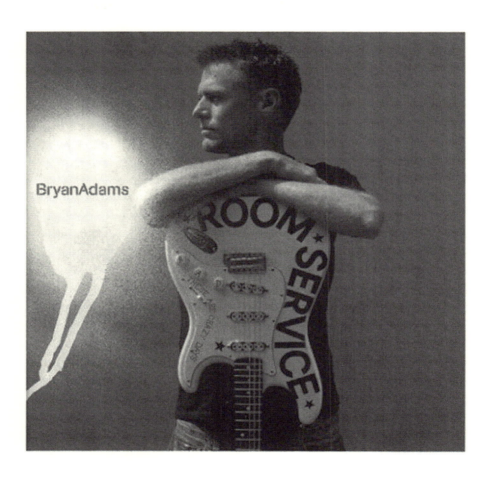

11

"Focus on the music, the songs – those are the most important parts of what you do, and ultimately, they're the things that will carry you along".

- Speaking to Joe Bosso, *Music Radar*, 2010

Adams released his tenth studio album, *11*, in March 2008. He considers the *Sprit* soundtrack to be his tenth album hence the name, *11*, for this particular release, which was his first new batch of material since 2005's *Colour Name Kubrick*.

"I go into a record with essentially same feeling I have towards all of them", he told Dominick A. Miserandino of *The Celebrity Café* in 2008. "I don't think this one changes my feeling towards it. It's my new work. I'm trying to tell everybody about it and then get on to the next one".

11 contains eleven tracks and despite the album's name and the amount of tracks there are no hidden messages or meanings. Much of the album was written on tour as with *Room Service* – whenever he had a spare moment in the hotel room or backstage before a gig he'd work on some vocals or overdubs and such.

"Recording on tour is easy", he said to Courtney Laura of *Reverb Online*, "I've done a few albums like that, but getting out and seeing the city isn't usually the easiest thing. Rest is usually required".

11 was originally intended to be an acoustic album but as the songs progressed Adams experimented and changed some tempos and the album ended up being more of a laidback electric guitar album but a far cry from the fast rock sound of his earlier work. He wrote thirty songs in total and whittled them down to eleven for the final album but nineteen for the deluxe edition.

Four years had passed since *Room Service* and the album was largely produced by Adams with Mutt Lange producing two tracks: 'Thought We Have The Stars' and 'We Found What We Were Looking For'.

"Mutt is great to work with because he is committed to making sure the songs have the best of everything before they go out into the world", Adams told *Song Facts*' Carl Weiser in 2009. "We've had three number one records together and many good times, a true friend".

Jim Vallance, Eliot Kennedy, Gretchen Peters, Trevor Rabin and Robert John "Mutt" Lange received producing and writing credits. 'Flower Grown Wild' was reportedly written about the late singer Amy Winehouse. He played it down, though, as he told the *Daily Mail*'s Adrian Thrills in 2008: "It was inspired by an article in *Rolling Stone* about a porn star who committed suicide. I've played on the theme of tragic figures in the past, but 'Flower Grown Wild' is also about how we devour our stars".

Adams hadn't worked with Vallance since the late 1980s and had begun exchanging ideas via email from 2003 onwards. Vallance would send Adams some MP3 files by email for him to use in his recording sessions and they'd continue to exchange ideas and files online throughout the making of the album, and as a consequence it took long to make a song than it did back in the day.

'Tonight We Have The Stars' was one of the songs Adams and Vallance exchanged over email. It was later mixed by Bob Clearmountain at his studio in LA. The three would exchange comments via iChat about the song's final mix.

The album features a host of musicians, including but not limited to, Keith Scott (guitar), Colin Cripps (guitar and backing vocals), Gary Breit (Hammond organ, piano), Eliot Kennedy (bass, piano and backing vocals), Norm Fisher (bass), Robert John "Mutt" Lange (bass), Mickey Curry (drums), Pat Steward (drums and tambourine), Jim Vallance (drums) and Máire Breatnach (fiddle, viola).

"Like all of my albums", he said to *TNT Magazine* in 2013, "it's just a collection of the best songs I could write. Nothing more nothing less. I couldn't possibly choose a favourite track, as all 11 songs sit very well with me".

The album was ready by September 2007 though its release was delayed until March 2008 for Europe and May for the US. To promote the album Adams played an eleven day, eleven country European acoustic promotional tour called 11 Concerts, 11 Cities Tour. The shows featured only Adams' with his guitar and harmonica. The London gig on March 11 2008 was held at St. James Church in Piccadilly with the last show held in Copenhagen, Denmark on March 17. Adams went on the road with his acoustic guitar and supported Foreigner and Rod Stewart; his acoustic shows eventually led to the *Bare Bones* Tour.

"…musically, I've always been about rediscovery – in the '90s with *Unplugged*, in the '00s with a three-piece band and now *Bare Bones*", he explained to *Examiner*'s Alison Richter. "It keeps things interesting for yourself and for the audience".

11 debuted at Number 1 in Canada (his first Canadian Number 1 album since 1991's *Waking Up The Neighbors*). It peaked at Number 2 in Germany but in the US it only reached Number 80, which was still better than how *Room Service* fared. *11* was released in the US via an exclusive deal with Wal-Mart and was for sale in Wal-Mart stores and Sam's Club retail stores.

Adams told John Newlin of *Zimbio* in 2012 about his reasons for hooking up with Wal-Mart: "I mean, Wal-Mart came in and said, 'We'd like to order some records', and we thought, 'Great'. I know the Eagles have done it and it seemed like a good idea. The last time I drove down Sunset Strip there wasn't even a record shop. So I thought, 'Good plan' and they seemed enthusiastic and we're all on a page here. I think iTunes is going to have it at some point, but I don't know. I thought it was quite a good idea if my record was there. You know you can get your dog food, you can get a Bryan Adams CD and you can get a light bulb, all at the same time".

The album reached Number 80 on the *Billboard* 200 album charts but Number 1 in India and Switzerland.

Overall, *11* sold half a million copies which is hugely disappointing for an artists of Adams' stature and his sales had been declining for some time, though CD sales have gone down in general for all artists due to illegal downloading. Adams still remains universally popular and has a devoted fanbase around the world.

The album's first single was 'I Thought I'd Seen Everything'. 'Tonight We Have The Stars' and 'She's Got Away' were also issued as singles.

Reviews of the album were mixed to poor.

Amy O'Brian wrote in *The Vancouver Sun*: "There is plenty of motivational-speak on *11* that suggests Adams has either been doing some soul-searching or watching too much Oprah. It's cheesy and overdone, but the truth is that it just might give Adams his first hit in a decade".

People magazine's Chuck Arnold wrote: "There's nothing on the new Bryan Adams album that will erase the '80s memory of 'Summer of '69' or 'Run To You'. But the 11 songs on this CD – which is exclusively available at Wal-Mart and Sam's Club – show that, at 48, Adams is still capable of capturing the essence of young, unbridled love. Sure, the guy can get sappy, but he's always sincere".

JAM!'s Darryl Sterdan wrote: "…the production is simple yet tasteful, there's plenty of excellent slide guitar, cello and keyboard work and Adams still knows how to spin instantly memorable hooks and choruses. But in the end, it's just another predictably well-crafted set of superficial, cliche-filled numbers that don't really mean much".

Andrew McNeice expressed his thoughts on the album on his indispensable website *Melodicrock.com*: "Well, at the end of the day this isn't as bad as I first thought, but it still falls way short of expectations and even further short of my ideal Bryan Adams album. I guess fans have to be resigned to the fact that the days of *Reckless*, *Into The Fire*, *Cuts Like A Knife* and even *Waking Up The Neighbours* are so far gone, they ain't ever coming back. Once you get past that mindset and accept that Bryan Adams 2008 is a crooning balladeer, you can sit back and take in *11* for what it is – a selection of laid back pop ballads and mid-tempo adult contemporary tracks".

11 opens with 'Tonight We Have The Stars' is on repeated listens is an excellent track, very effective and evocative. 'I Thought I'd Seen Everything' is a modest ballad while 'I Ain't Losin' The Fight' is a catchy mid-paced toe-tapper with a strong chorus. 'Oxygen' is a typical Bryan Adams rocker of the modern day. It doesn't quite catch you despite a fairly effective riff and a chorus that tries to grab you. 'We Found What We Were Looking For' and 'Broken Wings' are both very average ballads though Adams gives an excellent vocal performance. 'Somethin' To Believe In' is an acoustic based number that offers nothing new while 'Mysterious Ways' heads down a similar middle of the road route. 'She's Got A Way' is a slightly more effective ballad than its predecessors. 'Flower Grown Wild' is a surprisingly fun song with an acoustic led rhythm and a memorable chorus. 'Walk On By' is a quiet, whispery slower number while 'The Way Of The World' is the closing number and a bonus track to boot, though nothing specially memorable.

11 is undoubtedly his weakest album and firmly cements him in the middle of the road category of seasoned singer-songwriters. He's always balanced rock songs with ballads but *11* is just a collection of too many slow numbers and a total lack of indelible riffs.

Adams announced via Twitter in 2009 that he had begun writing and recording material for a new album in Paris where he has a home.

To celebrate his success he was one of four musicians to be pictured on the second series of the Canadian Recording Artists Series issued by Canada Post Stamps in July 2009. Over one million Bryan Adams stamps were printed.

In 2009 he co, produced and sang the track 'You've Been A Friend To Me' for the Disney film *Old Dogs*.

In February, 2010 he released 'One World, One Flame' which was used as the theme song by the German TCV station ARD for their coverage of the Olympic Games in Vancouver. Also in that month Adams sung a duet with fellow Canadian Nelly Furtado called 'Bang The Drum' which was co-written with Jim Vallance for the opening ceremony of the 2010 Winter Olympic Games in Vancouver at the indoors DC Place Stadium.

Further special live performances continued when he performed at a party attended by (retired New York Rangers player) Wayne Gretzky and Pittsburgh Penguins) Jaromir Jagr. Adams sang the Canadian national anthem. He was also one of many popular artists to visit the Canadian Prime Minister Stephen Harper at his official residence which became a rather impromptu jam session. Adams was there to discuss the copyright laws in Canada.

Adams released the acoustic live album *Bare Bones* in November 2010, which was recorded at various countries on the *Bare Bones* Tour from May 27 to June 16 2010.

The album was certified Gold in India. It's quite a different album from anything he's done in the past. Playing songs like 'Cuts Like A Knife' and 'Straight From The Heart' on an acoustic guitar is different from having a full band.

Adams spoke to Sophie Gilbert of the *Washingtonian* in 2012 about the recording of the album: "Mostly in America, but some of it in Oslo. Originally it was going to be recorded in Oslo and we got it all set up and got out there, and throughout the night there was some drunk guy out there who kept going, 'I love you man! I really love you!' And he did it at the most inopportune moments – he wouldn't do it between songs, he'd wait till a really quiet moment. So I walked offstage thinking, 'I guess we'll have to go back and do it another night'".

Bare Bones is a refreshing album and far from being a gimmick, Adams is in terrific form. The production is spot on, giving the listener a close, intimate feeling. It's a raw, pure and back to basics sound stripping each song back to the bone. It also shows that Adams' skill these days is on stage rather than in the studio, at least onstage he is far more interesting and energetic. The setlist is refreshing and captivating as he sails through 'You've Been A Friend To Me', 'Here I Am', 'I'm Ready', 'Let's Make A

Night To Remember', 'It Ain't A Party If You Don't Come Round', '(Everything I Do) I Do It For You', 'Cuts Like A Knife', 'Please Forgive Me', 'Summer Of '69', 'Walk On By', 'Cloud Number Nine', 'It's Only Love', 'Heaven', 'The Right Place', 'The Way You Make Me Feel', 'The Only Thing That Looks Good On Me Is You', 'You're Still Beautiful To Me', 'Straight From The Heart', 'I Still Miss You…A Little Bit' and 'All For Love'.

Moving in 2011 and Adams became the first global star to perform in Nepal (specifically in Kathmandu) which was organized by the ODC Network (P) LTD. He also performed at the opening ceremony of the International Cricket Council's World Cup in Dhaka, Bangladesh on February 17, 2011. He played a solo set the next day for fans.

The *Bare Bones* Tour journeyed around packed venues in the US and Canada. In August Adams played Ruth Eckerd Hall in Clearwater, Florida. The shows were entirely solo though he had the help of keyboardist Gary Breit. "Gary joins me on about half the show", Adams told Alison Richter of *Examiner*. "He's amazing. He's worked with me about seven years and its way different to when we started, especially with the *Bare Bones* show. He really shines here. He's a great accompanist. Sometimes I think we sound like one instrument".

Gabe Echazabal and Tracy May reviewed the show for *Creative Loafing Tampa Bay*: "For two hours, Adams, without the aid of an opening act, treated a roomful of faithful fans to a vast array of hits, stories and anecdotes, with a few off-the-cuff moments scattered throughout. The most memorable was a totally impromptu duet with a diehard".

Adams' extensive setlist included hits from throughout his career and ran as follows: 'Run To You', 'How Do Ya Feel Tonight', 'Back To You', 'Here I Am', 'I'm Ready', 'This Time', 'Lonely Nights', 'Do I Have To Say The Words?', 'Let's Make A Night To Remember', 'Can't Stop This Thing We Started', 'Still Beautiful To Me', 'Heat Of The Night', 'Not Romeo Not Juliet', '(Everything I Do) I Do It For You', 'Cuts Like A Knife', 'If Ya Wanna Be Bad Ya Gotta Be Good', 'Please Forgive Me', 'Summer Of '69', 'Walk On By', 'Heaven', 'The Right Place' and 'The Only Thing That Looks Good On Me Is You' with a first encore of 'Somebody', 'You've Been A Friend To Me', 'Have You Ever Really Loved A Woman?' and 'I Still Miss You...A Little Bit' and a second and final encore of the classic 'Straight From The Heart'.

On November 20 he wrote and recorded music video for the dance track 'Tonight In Babylon' in Southwark, London for Loverush UK!. The day after he performed 'When You're Gone' on the TV talent show *The X Factor*.

In January 2012 he kicked off the twenty date Canadian tour Waking Up The Nation Tour to celebrate twenty years of *Waking Up The Neighbours*, one of his best known albums.

"You know what, I kind of think my voice is stronger than ever", he said to Nathan Wood of *MaxTV* in 2012. "When I hear about some of my contemporaries, my colleagues having trouble, I wonder because one of the things I don't do – I don't drink. I wonder how much alcohol has to do with paying the price of your voice, and I'm just throwing that out there because I have no way of justifying what I just said. I think taking care of yourself is a big part of taking care of your voice is all part in parcel".

In July he voiced the character of Jock, a dog, in the South African animated film *Jock Of The Bushveld*. He wrote two songs for the album, which, was retitled *Jock The Hero Dog* for American audiences, 'Way Oh' and 'By Your Side'.

In 2013 he wrote and sang on the track 'After All' with fellow Canadian Michael Buble for his album *To Be Loved*.

Adams released *Live At The Sydney Opera House* on CD and DVD in 2013, which was recorded on the *Bare Bones* Tour back in 2011. He continued to play *Bare Bones* shows to 2013. He played Hartford, Connecticut in December 2013. Donnie Moorehouse reviewed the gig for *Masslive*: "The songs were indicative of the era's pop-infused rock, three or four chords with a romantic sentiment attached and only the instrumentation indicating the genre as pop, rock, metal, or dance. Adams was the best of the bunch with a universal appeal and husky blues voice that still rings out in mid-80s form".

A CASUAL GUIDE TO THE MUSIC OF BRYAN ADAMS

He kept himself busy throughout 2014 by staying on the road. Jen Zoratti of *Winnipeg Free Press* reviewed Adams' gig at Centennial Concert Hall in Winnipeg in February: "Adams was affable and easygoing, even taking an unsolicited request for 'Back To You' and politely telling the rowdies in the crowd to shut up. (He's a nice Canadian boy, after all). His voice began wearing out a little about midway through the show, but its rawness (mostly) worked to his favour; a cover of Kris Kristofferson's 1970 hit 'Help Me Make It Through The Night' was given a gritty, whiskey-soaked weariness. Even Adams' cotton-candy rock hits – see: 'The Only Thing That Looks Good On Me Is You', which came later in the set – were elevated by the lighter, bare-bones touch. Predictably, the crowd went wild for 'Summer Of '69', though his slightly rushed rendition didn't rank among the night's strongest performances".

In 2014 he announced the 30th Anniversary *Reckless* Tour of the UK where he played in some of the country's biggest and most popular venues.

With eleven studio albums to his name and hundreds of songs Bryan Adams is one of the most successful singer-songwriters in popular music. It's interesting that despite his obvious lack of interest in making rock albums anymore he's still keen to play the old hits as well as revisit the albums that made him a household names with tours dedicated to the anniversaries of both *Reckless* and *Waking Up The Neighbours*.

While a cynic would say the reasons for those tours could be fiscally motivated he's still got the energy and charisma of a rock star half his age.

He is a terrific live performer and plays over a hundred shows a year, sure it's half of what he used to do but it's still more than what many of his peers can manage these days. He's far removed from the singer-songwriter he was in the 1980s and while many of us would love to hear one more great rock album from him there's no question that seeing him live remains a spectacle.

"I wouldn't change anything, well maybe I'd change the first 20 years and start after that!" he said to *TNT Magazine* in 2013. "I can't tell you how long the road is, it's never-ending. The journey never seems to end, it just transforms into something else. I always said if it started to feel like a job, I'd stop. Thankfully it hasn't become that and I still love making music".

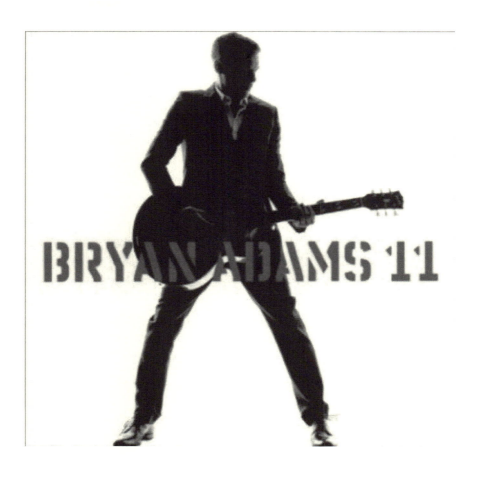

നോട്ട്

PART TWO

MISCELLANEOUS

TIMELINE

What follows is a selective timeline of important releases and events since 1980, the year Bryan Adams released his self-titled debut album. Wherever possible the exact date has been listed, otherwise just the month and year. This is a selective list.

1980s

1980

February 12 – *Bryan Adams* was released.

1981

July 21 – *You Want It, You Got It* was released.

1982

July 23 – Bryan Adams played at Summer Jam 1982 with Foreigner, Blue Öyster Cult, Joan Jett & The Blackhearts and others.

1983

January 10 – 'Run To You' was written.

January 18 – *Cuts Like A Knife* was released.

February – 'Straight From The Heart' was released as a single.

May 27 – 'Cuts Like A Knife' was released.

June 6-7 – 'Heaven' was recorded at The Power Station in NYC.

August – 'This Time' was released as a single.

1984

January 25 – Finished recording 'Summer Of '69'.

March – 'Diana' was written.

March 27 – Adams began recording *Run To You* in Vancouver.

September 21 – *Run To You* was mixed in NYC.

October 18 – 'Run To You' was released as a single.

November 5 – *Reckless* was released.

December – Adams launched the *Reckless* Tour.

1985

January – 'Heaven' was released to Canadian radio.

February 1 – Adams played a show at the Hollywood Palladium.

February – 'One Night Love Affair' was released to Canadian radio.

April – Adams finished a fifty date tour supporting Tina Turner in Europe.

April 9 – 'Heaven' was released as a single.

June – 'Summer Of '69' was released as a single.

July 13 – Adams performed at Live Aid at the JFK Stadium in Philadelphia.

October – Adams finished the World Wide In '85 Tour.

1986

June – Adams took part in the two week long 'A Conspiracy Of Hope' organised by Amnesty International.

1987

March – 'Heat Of The Night' was released as a single.

March 30 – *Into The Fire* was released.

June – Adams performed at the fifth annual Prince's Trust Rock Gala in London.

1988

July 3 – Adams played at the Rock Werchter festival in Werchter, Belgium.

1989

August – Adams wrote 'When The Night Comes' with Vallance, and Diane Warren also which was featured on the Joe Cocker opus *One Night Of Sin* and when released as a single, it reached the US Top 20.

1990s

1990

July 21 – Adams took part in *The Wall – Live In Berlin* with Roger Waters and guests to celebrate the fall of the Berlin Wall.

1991

June 14 – *Robin Hood: Prince Of Thieves* was released in US cinemas.

June – '(Everything I Do) I Do It For You' was released as a single.

September 24 – *Waking Up The Neighbours* was released.

October 2 – 'Can't Stop This Thing We Started' was released as a single.

October 4 – Adams launched the Waking Up The World Tour.

November 10 – 'There Will Never Be Another Tonight' was released as a single.

December 18 – Adams played the first of two shows in Reykjavik, Iceland.

1992

January 10 – Adams played a sold out show the Ritz in NYC.

January 13 – The Canadian leg of the Waking Up The World Tour commenced.

January 31 – The Canadian leg of the Waking Up The World Tour ended.

February – Adams played shows in Australia and New Zealand.

February 21 – Adams played the first of six shows in Japan.

June – The Waking Up The World Tour was taken to Europe.

July – 'Do I Have To Say The Words?' was released as a single.

July – Adams played his first ever shows in Hungary and Turkey.

September – Adams returned to the US as part of the Waking Up the World Tour.

December – The US leg of the Waking Up The World Tour drew to a close.

1993

February – Adams played shows in Asia.

March – Adams returned to the US fort more shows.

April 24 – Adams performed at the high-profile Farm Aid VI concert alongside Johnny Cash, Willie Nelson and Ringo Starr.

May – The US leg of the Waking Up The World tour ended the tour.

November 2 – 'Please Forgive Me' was released as a single.

November 9 – *So Far So Good* was released.

November 12 – *The Three Musketeers* was released in US cinemas.

November 16 – 'All For Love' was released as a single.

1994

January 25 – Adams kicked off the *So Far So Good* Tour in Australia at Perth Entertainment Centre.

1995

April 14 – 'Have You Ever Really Loved A Woman?' was released as a single.

November 3 – 'Rock Steady' with Bonnie Raitt was released as a single.

1996

May 7 – 'The Only Thing That Looks Good On Me Is You' was released as a single.

June 4 – *18 Til I Die* was released.

August 17 – 'Let's Make A Night To Remember' was released as a single.

November – 'Star' was released as a single.

November 5 – 'I Finally Found Someone' with Barbara Streisand was released as a single.

1997

April – '18 Til I Die' was released as a single.

July 27 – Adams played to 70,000 at Wembley Stadium.

September 26 – Adams recorded *MTV Unplugged*.

November 21 – 'Back To You' was released as a single.

December 9 – *MTV Unplugged* was released.

1998

October 27 – *One A Day Like Today* was released.

November – 'On A Day Like Today' was released as a single.

November 30 – 'When You're Gone' was Mel C was released as a single.

1999

April 18 – 'Cloud Number Nine' was released as a single.

October – Adams joined Tina Turner onstage for her 60th anniversary birthday show at the Royal Albert Hall. They sang 'It's Only Love'.

November 15 – *The Best Of Me* was released in the US.

November 15 – 'The Best Of Me' was released as a single.

2000s

2000

March 6 – 'Don't Give Up' by Chicane with Bryan Adams was released as a single.

November 27 – Adams played onstage with The Who at the Royal Albert Hall, which was issued on DVD.

2001

January 19 – Kicked started a new tour at Edinburgh Playhouse.

2002

May 14 – *Spirit: Stallion Of The Cimarron* soundtrack was released in the US.

May 24 – *Spirit: Stallion Of The Cimarron* was released in US cinemas.

June 11 – 'Here I Am' was released as a single.

2003

June 17 – *Live At The Budokan* was released in the US.

2004

September 13 – 'Open Road' was released as a single.

September 20 – *Room Service* was released in the UK.

November 29 – 'Flying' was released as a single.

2005

January 29 – Adams performed at the CBC Benefit concert on Toronto for the victims of the 2004 Indian Ocean earthquake.

March 28 – 'Room Service' was released as a single.

May – *Room Service* was released in the US.

October 18 – *Anthology* was released in the US.

2006

April – Adams was inducted into the Canadian Music Hall Of Fame at the Juno Awards.

May 15 – Adams attended the Hope Foundation charity event in London.

July 31 – Adams performed a free concert with Billy Joel at the Coliseum, in Rome, Italy.

2007

December 5 – Performed at the Eesti Näituste messikeskus, Tallinn in Estonia.

2008

January 28 – 'I Thought I'd' Seen Everything' was released as a single.

February 28 – Adams performed at the One Night Live charity event at the Air Canada Centre in Toronto.

March 17 – *11* was released in the US.

May 30 – 'Thought We Have The Stars' was released as a single.

September – 'She's Got A Way' was released as a single.

September 19 – Adams performed a concert in Tbilisi to support the peace in Georgia.

2009

July 2 – Adams was one of four musicians from the Canadian Recording Artist Series to be featured on a series of Canadian stamps.

November 14 – Adams performed at the Wild And Live event at the Royal Albert Hall in London, which was organised by the Born Free Foundation.

December – Adams wrote and recorded 'You've Been A Friend To Me' for the Disney film *Old Dogs*, which was released as a single.

2010s

2010

January 13 – Adams received the Allan Waters Humanitarian Award.

February – Adams released 'One World, One Flame' which was used by the German TV station ARD for their coverage of the Olympic Games. It was released as a single.

February 12 – Adams performed 'Bang The Drum' with Nelly Furtado at the 2010 Winter Olympic Games in Vancouver.

May 1 – Adams was handed the Governor General's Performing Arts Award.

August 31 – *Icon* was released in the US.

October 29 – *Bare Bones* was released in the US.

2011

February 19 – Adams was the first international artists to perform in Kathmandu, Nepal.

March – Adams was inducted into the Hollywood Walk Of Fame.

November 19 – Adams wrote and recorded 'Tonight In Babylon' for Loverush UK!.

November 20 – Adams performed 'When You're Gone' on the UK show, *The X-Factor*.

2012

June – Adams won the Lead Award in Germany for his fashion work. He'd won it for the first time in 2006.

July – Adams voiced the character Jock in the South African animated film *Jock Of The Bushveld*.

October – Adams first book of photographs, Exposed, was published by Steidl.

2013

November – Adams published *Wounded – The Legacy Of War*, a photographic book about war.

2014

November 13 – Adam began the UK leg of the 30th Anniversary *Reckless* Tour in Nottingham.

November 26 – The UK leg finished in London.

December – Adams took the 30th Anniversary *Reckless* Tour to Berlin, Stuttgart, Cologne and Munich.

A CASUAL GUIDE TO THE MUSIC OF BRYAN ADAMS

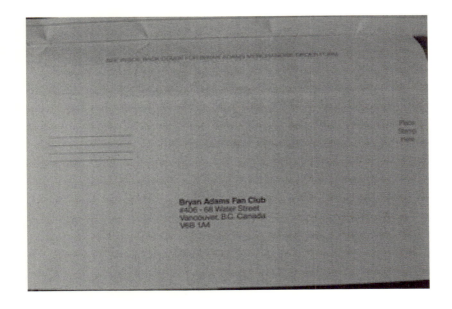

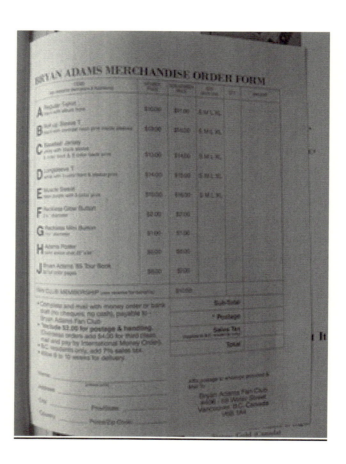

A CASUAL GUIDE TO THE MUSIC OF BRYAN ADAMS

ASSORTED REVIEWS

The following reviews were written for various magazines/websites that I have contributed to in the past. These are not the printed copies but my own revised versions. These reviews were written at the time of the respective releases and my opinions have since changed in some respects.

BRYAN ADAMS – *ANTHOLOGY* (Album, Polydor)

More comprehensive than 1999's *Best Of Me*, this is the Canadians singer's first two CD anthology of his twenty-five year career. It covers all his hits (and some lesser known gems) from 1980 up to 2005. And encompasses ten British Top 10 hit singles, two of which made it to the revered Number 1 spot.

Surprisingly, it hasn't been an easy ride for Adams, not everything in his career is worthwhile. The early stuff like 'Run To You' and 'It's Only Love' (with Tina Turner) are good solid rock songs but then he went even more lovey-dovey with the sickening sentimentally of '(Everything I Do) I Do It For You'. With his working class background and songs like 'Summer Of '69' he was a worthy rival to Bruce Springsteen but the later soundtrack songs were like Phil Collins cast offs. The excellent *18 Til I Die* (the title track from the superb Mutt Lange produced album) remains shamefully neglected and his latest efforts such as 'Open Road' from the 2005 album *Room Service* are often bland and unchallenging. Yet 'When Your Gone' with Melanie C is a hoot. There are two new tracks included here that don't jump out literally.

Adams needs to gain back that harder, edgy working class sound that he started out with if he is to remain exciting. *Anthology* is a thoughtful and entertaining collection of a chequered career where most the rock songs are definitely worth paying attention to but some of the romantic ballads are a little iffy, which is ironic seeing as is he is mostly famous for them these days.

BRYAN ADAMS – 'OPEN ROAD' (Single, Polydor)

UK Release Date: 13th September 2004

You can always rely on Bryan Adams to make the kind of soft rock that is good fun to listen to when you're bored yet even more enjoyable when you're drunk. He hasn't evolved much since his 1983 breakthrough single, 'Straight From The Heart'; he is like a stray dog who doesn't seem to fit in anywhere, you don't want to kick him to move him out of the way because your so use to his presence.

'Open Road' is taken from the Canadian singer's forthcoming album, *Room Service* – his first since 2002's sickly sweet *Spirit: Stallion*

Of The Cimarron. It's a likable track that carries his most distinctive ingredients with a spoonful of aplomb: the husky voice, catchy chorus and smooth well-polished riffs, and there is even a nifty harmonica spot in the middle.

'Open Road' runs like a calm flow of water and is friendly enough without causing too much nausea. In fact, if you sat down and closed your eyes it would feel like the mid '80s again.

BRYAN ADAMS – M.E.N ARENA (22/10/04)

At the age of 45 and still retaining his infectious boyish charm, energetic stage demeanour and gravelly voice; the Canadian soft rock crooner, Bryan Adams annoyingly continues to hold onto the enviable position of attracting hordes of attractive women to his successful arena tours.

The teenage heartthrob turned all-round mums favorite is touring old Blighty to promote his latest Sunday-afternoon-radio-rock-opus, *Room Service*; and begins tonight's proceedings with the title track quickly followed by his current single, 'Open Road'.

What followed was a two hour collection of terrifically entertaining AOR filled with favorites like 'Summer Of '69', 'Run To You', 'Kid's Wanna Rock', 'Can't Stop This Thing' and of course the obligatory, chart domineering'(Everything I Do) I Do It For You'.

Besides three large screens and an elaborate lightning scheme, the stage was free of any ostentatious stage props or centerpieces yet the dedicated audience was content and actually euphoric, with just Adams and his band performing on a bland stage.

Before he burst into 'It's Only Love', which he originally sang with Tina Turner, Adams explained that it's been twenty years since his pivotal *Reckless* album and his first tour of the UK as support during Turner's *Private Dancer* tour. Since then it's been a largely smooth ride despite a few recent bumps but his ability as a fantastic live performer has never diminished.

Although much of his contemporary work considerably lacks the hard, sweaty upbeat tempo of his '80s efforts, the ravenous crowd sang to literally every song with considerable aplomb. After two encores Bryan Adams walked off stage a true king – if only for a night.

BRYAN ADAMS - M.E.N ARENA (08/05/07)

Room Service, Bryan Adams' last studio album, was released in 2004 so with nothing new what was the point in this tour? He admitted that a fresh album was supposed to be finished and in shops but he is still writing and recording new material. Obviously that is going to result in another UK tour sometime soon which delighted the adoring fans in the packed arena.

A CASUAL GUIDE TO THE MUSIC OF BRYAN ADAMS

So basically it was a night filled with his big hits and charming soft rock- radio friendly tunes. To the confusion of the crowd, Adams and his band opened the set on a smaller stage in the centre of the standing area but it wasn't until the second song 'Can't Stop This Thing We Started' that things really got going although a solo acoustic version of 'Please Forgive Me' was a bit of a bore after such an exciting start. He played for two-and-a-half hours and (literally) ran through all the big hits: 'Run To You', 'Cuts Like A Knife', 'It's Only Love', 'Summer Of '69', '18 Til I Die' and that other one which doesn't need mentioning. He also did a walkabout amongst the crowd during 'Best Of Me' and did his usual thing of inviting a member of the audience to sing with him during 'When You're Gone'.

A rock show doesn't come much more entertaining than this.

A CASUAL GUIDE TO THE MUSIC OF BRYAN ADAMS

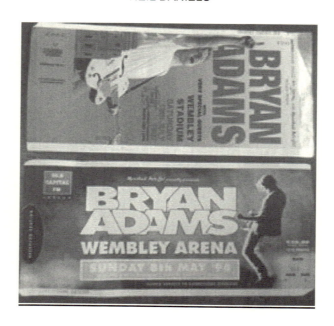

A CASUAL GUIDE TO THE MUSIC OF BRYAN ADAMS

TRIVIA

What follows are some bits of trivia and information that Bryan Adams fans may find interesting. The trivia listed here is related to his music, fashion, photography and philanthropic work.

Reckless is the best-selling Canadian album of all time. He was handed the Diamond Sales Award for the opus, which was a first for a Canadian.

Adams was inducted into the Canadian Music Hall Of Fame in 2006.

For his services to music Adams was handed the CM (Member Of The Order Of Canada) on April 20, 1998 and then the CO (Officer Of The Order Of Canada) on May 6, 1998.

He was inducted on to the Canadian Walk Of Fame in Toronto in 1998.

He was inducted on the Hollywood Walk Of Fame For Recording at 6752 in Hollywood Boulevard on March 21, 2001.

The song 'Diana' caused minor news as some suspected it was about Princess Diana. Years later Adams' ex-girlfriend alleged that he had an affair with the late princess in 1996 after she split from Prince Charles.

'(Everything I Do) I Do It For You' was recorded in Spanish in 1992.

'Here I Am' was recorded in French in 2007.

Artists who have sung Bryan Adams penned songs include Acker Bilk, Brandy, Laura Branigan, Eric Carmen, Richard Clayderman, Joe Cocker, Billy Ray Cyrus, Neil Diamond, Celine Dion, Johnny Hallyday, Lisa Hartman, Highway 101, Engelbert Humperdinck, KISS, Jack Jones, the Law, Henry Mancini, Randy Meisner, Lorrie Morgan, Anne Murray, Luciano Pavarotti, Bonnie Raitt, the Rovers, Neal Schon, Barbra Streisand, John Tesh, Tina Turner, Bonnie Tyler, Uriah Heep, Bob Welch, Roger Whittaker, John Williams, Trisha Yearwood, and Zamfir.

Between 1976 and 1977 he was the lead singer of the band Sweeney Todd.

Ironically, during a gig at the Winnipeg Arena in 1998 Adams made a remark about the venue's portrait of Queen Elizabeth II, commenting that he'd never seen her smile. Fast forwarded to 2002 and he photographed the

Queen on her Golden Jubilee with the Queen smiling. The photograph was used on a Canadian stamp.

Waking Up The Neighbours was declared "non-Canadian" in 1991 because it was co-written with Mutt Lane who is British. It's reported that he refuses to attend the Juno Awards because of it. The laws have since been changed.

In 2005 a British poll stated '(Everything I Do) I Do It For You' is the most popular song played at British weddings.

'(Everything I Do) I Do It For You' was Number 1 for sixteen weeks in the UK.

His birthday, November 5, is the same birthday as Ryan Adams.

Adams has been involved with Greenpeace since the 1980s and has been involved in various campaigns. He was involved in the creation of the Southern Antarctic Ocean sanctuary for whales.

Adams reportedly declined to let the producers of *Top Gun*, the 1986 Tom Cruise movie, to use his song 'Only The Strong Survive' from *Into The*

Fire because he felt the film glorified war.

He attended the same Vancouver high school as *Back To The Future* star Michael J. Fox.

His manager is Bruce Allen.

'Heaven' is his only Number 1 not to have been written for the cinema.

Adams has been nominated for seventeen Grammy awards.

Adams has two children with Alicia Grimaldi, trustee and co-founder of The Bryan Adams Foundation, Mirabella Bunny Adams and Lula Rosylea.

Adams played a gas station attendant in the 1989 Clint Eastwood film *Pink Cadillac* and a hallucination of himself in the 2002 film *House Of Fools*.

He collects the work of the West Coast artist Emily Carr who painted in the early 20th Century.

Adams pulls out members of the audience to sing 'Summer Of '69' and

'When You're Gone'; with him which is reminiscent of Bruce Springsteen and 'Dancing In The Dark'.

Adams is a vegan.

Adams is a vocal animal rights activist and supports the PETA (People For The Ethical Treatment Of Animals). He writes letters and takes photographs for them.

He owns The Bryan Adams Foundation, which is mostly funded by his high profile photographic endeavours.

Adams has been involved in Live Aid, Farm Aid, Born Free Foundation, Amnesty International and Prince's Trust amongst other high-profile charities.

He has sold over 100 million albums worldwide.

He has won twenty Juno Awards with fifty-six nominations.

He is a successful photographer and has photographed Annie Lennox, Arcade Fire, Morrissey, Lana Del Rey, The Who, Sting, Shania Twain,

Plácido Domingo, Mick Jagger, Ray Charles, Sarah McLachlan, Tina Turner, Rod Stewart, Robert Plant, Take That, Joss Stone, Celine Dion, Billy Idol, Moby, Lindsay Lohan, Amy Winehouse, Peter Gabriel, Bryan Ferry, Lenny Kravitz, Die Antwoord and Boy George.

He begun taking photography seriously in the early 2000s. He told *The Daily Telegraph*'s David Jenkins: "My focus was music, and I was 100 per cent blinkered. And then about 10 years ago, I pulled the blinkers off. I'd been round the world a hundred times and had started to forget where I'd been. I knew I'd been there: it said it on the tour map. I could remember the name of the city but I couldn't remember what it was like – it was a massive blur. I was on tour for three, nearly four years, and people in the crew were getting married and divorced, and there was this Peyton Place/Somerset Maugham backstage scenario going on, and I thought, 'Right: this has got to stop'".

His photography has been published in British *Vogue*, *L'uomo Vogue*, *Harper's Bazaar*, *Esquire*, *Interview* magazine and *i-D*, among many other high profile magazines.

He has photographed advertising campaigns for Guess Jeans, Escada, Sand, Converse, Montblanc, John Richmond and Fred Perry.

A CASUAL GUIDE TO THE MUSIC OF BRYAN ADAMS

He has published two books of photography: *Exposed* and *Wounded – The Legacy Of War*. He's also published three books of portraits: *Made In Canada* (1999), *Haven* (2000) and *American Women* (2005).

As a photographer he supports *Hear The World*, which raises global awareness of hearing loss.

The 2011 posthumous release by Amy Winehouse, *Lioness: Hidden Treasures*, has a cover by Adams.

He has had two motorbike accidents: in 2000 in Jamaica he hurt his knee and bruised his hip and ribcage after he crashed into a tree. In 2003 in London he was shot in the back with an air riffle which left a whole in his leather jacket.

A school in Dallas, Texas is called Bryan Adams High School which opened in 1957, two years before his birth. The school is named after a prominent Dallas figure.

Both his parents are British though he is Canadian and lives in the UK and has been for over twenty years.

He owns a studio in Vancouver called The Warehouse.

He owns a house in Chelsea, London and a flat in Paris. His London home was originally three houses, one of which was a pub called The King's Arms. But he slowly bought them all over the years and now he owns what you could only assume to be a rather large London home.

He supports Chelsea football team.

A CASUAL GUIDE TO THE MUSIC OF BRYAN ADAMS

A CASUAL GUIDE TO THE MUSIC OF BRYAN ADAMS

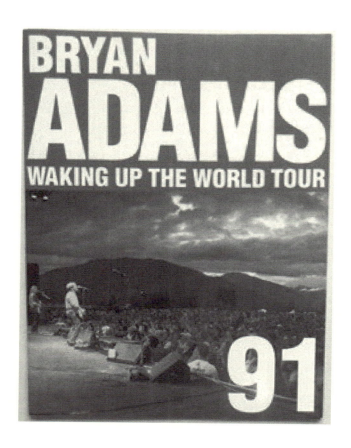

A CASUAL GUIDE TO THE MUSIC OF BRYAN ADAMS

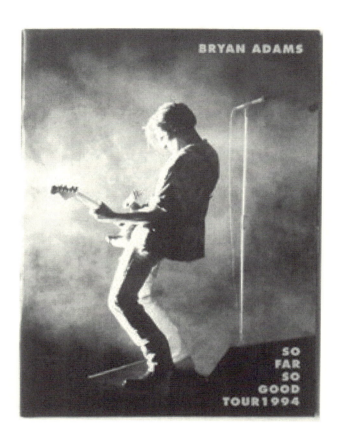

A CASUAL GUIDE TO THE MUSIC OF BRYAN ADAMS

A CASUAL GUIDE TO THE MUSIC OF BRYAN ADAMS

A CASUAL GUIDE TO THE MUSIC OF BRYAN ADAMS

NEIL DANIELS

BRYAN ADAMS IN HIS OWN WORDS

Here are some press quotes from the man himself.

'I don't generally write at home. I usually have to go away and lock myself up and get away from everything to write. But yeah, when I write, the first instrument I pick up is an acoustic'.
- Speaking to Joe Bosso, *Music Radar*, 2010

"The difference between the '80s and the '90s was radio just played my slower numbers instead of the rockers, so I had a cascade of slow songs that were hits instead".
- Speaking to Deborah Wagner, *PopEntertainment*, 2005

"I'm always performing. It is neverending. I've done at least 10 days a month for the past 10 years".
- Speaking to Phil Roura, *New York Daily News*, 2008

"I was in England on my own, trying to get A&M Records interested in my career but they told me to not even think about it. One guy said I would never make it in the UK, and should just go home. That gave me a real 'fuck you' attitude. It made me determined to succeed".

- Speaking to Adrian Thrills, *Daily Mail*, 2008

"In terms of ideas, I just try to create ideas that work really well in the live context. I always play things with a band so I try and create music that is great for live shows. I kind of feel like all of my work sort of flows into each other".

- Speaking to John Newlin, *Zimbio*, 2008

"If anything it's simply another creative outlet, much like learning to master an instrument. There is so much to learn, even if it's empirically. People always ask me for advice on songs and how to do it, and I always say play them live. You have to get out of the studio and perform them to figure out if they really work or not".

- Speaking to Carl Wiser, *Song Facts*, 2009

"I go into a record with essentially same feeling I have towards all of them. I don't think this one changes my feeling towards it. It's my new work. I'm trying to tell everybody about it and then get on to the next one".

- Speaking to Dominick A. Miserandino, *The Celebrity Café*, 2008

"Don't sign anything and if you have to – get a good lawyer first. Don't sign anything over to any dodgy managers or production companies, because unless they manage the Rolling Stones you'll get ripped off for sure. If they are good people, they won't ask for your publishing. That's actually a great judge of if they are creeps or not. Remember the most important thing about any song deals: they need you a lot more than you need them".

- Speaking to Dale Kawashima, *Songwriter Universe*, 2013

"You know what I really would like to do. I always just wanted to be the singer or the bass player in the band. I'd love to have a band, where I was obviously the singer, but where it wasn't me, it wasn't my name. That's why you never see anything about me. I've never been enamoured by the idea of being a celebrity".

- Speaking to Simon Hattenstone, *The Guardian*, 2002

"Music is just such... it's not therapy, but it's a release, it's a joy, it's a pleasure. And it's a job – which is weird, because I don't think of it as a job".

- Speaking to David Jenkins, *The Daily Telegraph*, 2008

"I was eighteen and a loudmouth. If I would've been a loudmouth, an eighteen year old punk with no good songs, they would've told me to take a walk. I signed for nothing. I signed for one dollar. That's the way it worked. At the time I needed to prove myself".

- Speaking to Gary James, *Classic Bands*, 1982

"I'm the worst judge if whether a song's a hit or not. I never knew. I only record songs that I felt good about. So, if I felt like 'That feels pretty good, I'll go and record it in the studio and see how it goes'. But I had no reference and clearly no crystal ball to know whether or not it would be a hit. I'm still rubbish at it".

- Speaking to Nathan Woods, *Max TV*, 2012

"Social media is a giant distraction to the ultimate aim, which is honing your craft as a songwriter. There are people who are exceptional at it, however, and if you can do both things, then that's fantastic, but if you are a writer, the time is better spent on a clever lyric than a clever tweet".

- Speaking to Alison Richter, *Examiner*, 2012

"Recording on tour is easy, I've done a few albums like that, but getting out and seeing the city isn't usually the easiest thing. Rest is usually required".

- Speaking to Courtney Laura, *Reverb Online*, 2013

"I'm not completely vegan, I will accept tiny amounts of butter and I normally scrape off cheese when it's on top of pasta or something... I completely stopped eating dead creatures in 1989".

- Speaking to June Bird, *Animal Liberation Front*, 2000

"You need to be able to write your own songs and believe in yourself when nobody else does. In fact, having a thick skin is important because very few people will give two shits about someone with weird hair and dodgy dress sense looking for a record deal".

- Speaking to Hester Lacey, *FT Magazine*, 2013

"I always had a little bit of interest in it [photography], but never really considered taking it seriously because I was too obsessed with my music. Eventually what happened was I ended up taking photographs of friends and they really liked them, and other friends asked me to take pictures of them. One thing led to the next, and the

next thing I knew my pictures were getting published, and now I'm busy with that and my two other tours, as well".

- Speaking to Sophie Gilbert, *Washingtonian*, 2013

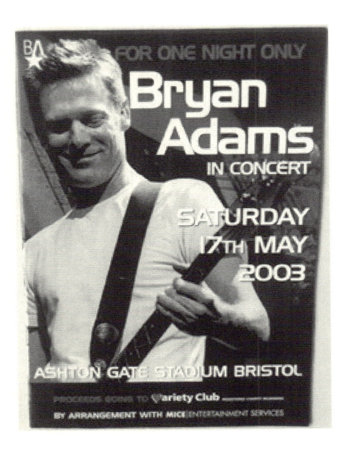

A CASUAL GUIDE TO THE MUSIC OF BRYAN ADAMS

NEIL DANIELS

ROCK SCRIBES TALK BRYAN ADAMS

Here are some thoughts on Bryan Adams music and live shows from fellow rock scribes and rock fans...

DEZ & MICK/BAILEY BROTHERS (*ROCK UNITED*): "Bryan Adams pre 1983? Never heard of him but one day the song 'Cuts Like A Knife' came on the radio (that was a mechanical device that you could tune in to frequencies and hear music played over the airwaves by radio stations). So we both immediately thought who's this Bryan Adams geezer who has that early Rod Stewart type growly voice? He looked like someone who had just enlisted into the army cadets rather than a rock star with his short hair; if he pulled up at your door and said he was the plumber you would have believed him. Mick got a copy of the song *Cuts Like A Knife* and we hammered the rock clubs with it. The album wasn't great but the follow up *Reckless* was a cracking album, 'Run To You' was a particular favourite with the UK fans but it was 'Summer Of 69' that was most requested.

Bryan did a song with Tina Turner 'It's Only Love' the last single release from *Reckless* I believe; that was a good collaboration and a successful one. The album is crammed with great songs it was definitely the global launch pad that catapulted Bryan Adams into the main stream and racked up a very impressive twelve million sales. Bryan always looked comfortable on stage and something usually over looked is that he is a very competent musician. Mick has fond memories of Bryan joining Roger Walters of Pink Floyd on stage in Berlin (*The Wall* concert): 'I have always been a big Pink Floyd fan but was surprised to see Bryan Adams on stage with Roger Walters. They did 'Empty Spaces' / 'What Shall We Do Now'. Adams also sung 'Young Lust' which was originally scheduled for Rod Stewart to perform but he couldn't make it in the end'.

A stand out gig for the Bailey's is when we were guest for Bryan Adams at Manchester City's old Maine Road ground, the date was July 7 1992; the line-up was Little Angels, Squeeze, Extreme and headlined by Bryan Adams. After performing a killer live set everyone was chanting for an encore and waiting for him to come back on stage, this mini circle appeared about half way down the pitch near the players tunnel with like a small drum kit on it, all of a sudden Bryan Adams jumped up and did a little set on it right in the middle of the crowd it was awesome and the first time we had seen the mini stage set up done. It was like he was saying, 'Yeah, I can do the big stage but happy on a pub stage too'. He's absolutely flawless live and another example of an artiste that can attract a diverse audience. You can't ignore a rock star who can stay at the top of the British singles chart for sixteen weeks with '(Everything I Do) I Do It For You', a great ballad and the album *Waking Up The Neighbours* must have clocked up sixteen million album sales but then again many said it was an album lined up for Def Leppard. It certainly had all the hall marks of a Leppard album with songs like 'Thought I'd Died And Gone To Heaven' and 'House Arrest' but that's the genius that is producer Robert John 'Mutt' Lange. For all its commercial success many Bryan Adam fans would still put *Reckless* before it as its more organic Adams as *Waking Up The Neighbours* was definitely written for a specific audience but sounds even more dated though it came many years later about 1991. Strangely enough a Bryan Adams unplugged album is currently taking centre stage on the car system and my daughter who is eight years-old keeps asking me to play track one 'Summer Of 69'. It goes to show how appealing Bryan's music is to all ages. Bryan Adams is a genuine nice bloke and great artist, he still looks like the plumber but now there are millions of house wives who would love him to knock on their door and sort their plumbing out".

ROB EVANS (*CLASSIC ROCK PRESENTS AOR*): "Back in '83 when Adams released his third offering, the punchy *Cuts Like A Knife*, he was subjected to the kind of character assassination that would have ended the careers of lesser men. Leading the charge was *Melody Maker* with, 'Exquisitely asinine drivel, second rate Saccharine rock', whilst *Creem* made it personal with, 'If I were Bryan Adams, I think I would see Nick

A CASUAL GUIDE TO THE MUSIC OF BRYAN ADAMS

Gilder haunting my dreams, and a million other scrumptious boys with photogenic faces and fixations on jukebox pop'.

It didn't bode well for his career, never mind any subsequent releases. But as we know the world of music is littered with artists who've been the subject of a critical mauling, only to bounce back with the album that defines them, Adams would prove to be no different.

Entering Little Mountain Studios – in Vancouver, Canada – with Bob Clearmountain at the helm, Adams took the best part of six months to create an album that would dominate the charts for the next year. It yielded seven singles, it could have been the entire album as there's not one bad song on it.

At this point in time I'd only remotely heard of Bryan Adams, I'd seen his albums but they didn't interest me. It was only when I was on my weekly trip to Penny Lane records, in Chester, that my love for *Reckless* began. It was thrust into my hand, as were a lot of Import albums in those days, by the ever eager Stewart, a curly haired aficionado of all things rock, with the immortal words, 'This is right up your street'.

He wasn't wrong, he rarely was, as tracks like the immemorial 'Run To You' and the saviour of many a wedding disco, 'Summer Of '69', would prove. These were the big hitters, the obvious choices as singles, and the songs that would become a staple of every Bryan Adams concert since '84.

But there was more to this album than the obvious choices, as the likes of 'One Night Love Affair' and 'Long Gone' would prove. The balladic 'Heaven' was a forerunner to that crime against music, '(Everything I Do), I Do For You', whilst 'Kids Wanna Rock' and 'Ain't Gonna Cry' showed that Adams was capable of adding muscle to his melody. On 'It's Only Love' Adams teamed up with Tina Turner, a pairing that toured the UK as part of Turner's *Private Dancer* tour of '85, a tour I missed because there was no way I was going to be seen at a Tina Turner gig.

Its plaudits have been many, including being voted into the *Kerrang!* '100 Greatest Heavy Metal Albums Of All Time' and the 'Top 100 Canadian Albums', but did it appease the critics on its day of release? Some things never change as *Melody Maker* went for the throat, 'You wonder how many hours of MTV and AOR radio monitoring went into the creation of this' and *Rolling Stone* dismissed it as, 'Generic rock 'n' roll, long on formal excellence but short on originality'.

The truth is that *Reckless* is a timeless album. Stack it up against the likes of *Hysteria* or *1987* and, unlike the aforementioned, it still sounds fresh to this very day. It's thanks to *Reckless* that we can forgive him for the Mutt Lange years, and the men in tights soundtrack abomination that was '(Everything I Do)…' It's thirty years-old this year, a celebration in itself".

NIKK GUNNS (*GET READY TO ROCK*): "Having heard the veritable onslaught of hit singles on the radio for a few years, it was in the mid to late '80s that I first saw Bryan Adams live, and I have attended every UK tour since – you could say that I am a bit of a fan. From his early work with Sweeney Todd, through to *Bare Bones* and on to this year's 30th Anniversary of *Reckless* (yes, 30 years – where did that go?!) Adams has given us years of great songs and great gigs. You also get the sense that the way his many fans feel about him is the same way that he feels about them, a genuinely rare quality these days. My favourite Bryan Adams story may or may not be myth but it is said that the vocal demo for the massively successful '(Everything I Do) I Do It For You' was so good that it ended up being the one used on the album-and on countless stereos around the world. Legend. Special mention must also be made of long-time sidekick Keith Scott – who, quite simply, is one of the most underrated guitarists of all time. Here's to many more years of great music from Bryan Adams".

ANDREW HAWNT (*POWERPLAY: ROCK & METAL MAGAZINE*): "It's hard for some people to think beyond a certain Number 1 single when they think of Bryan Adams. I get that. The song in question was Number 1 in the charts for roughly a century and a half, or at least that's what it felt like.

For a time, the Number 2 slot in the charts (back when the charts actually had some cultural worth) had to become a surrogate top spot as it got to the point where everyone just expected that song to be at the top for all time to come.

The thing is, Bryan Adams was never just about ballads. He had always primarily been a rock artist, attaining something of a more party-rock Bruce Springsteen vibe about him as the years wore on. Albums like the iconic *Reckless* may have had an air of era-specific pop rock, but the emphasis was always on the rock rather than the pop. But then came that damn song from the *Robin Hood* movie with Kevin Costner's mullet in it and everyone forgot about songs like 'Run To You' for a while and focused on a ballad with a video shot in a forest.

Bryan had become the establishment with that video and THAT song, which did propel him ever further into the stratosphere career-wise, but it also harmed what credibility he had thanks to its phenomenal success, leaving him with the unenviable task of coming up with material that wouldn't just be judged against past glories.

It wasn't really until he did the MTV *Unplugged* show that he regained some ground and people remembered that he was a musician and not just the bloke who broke the charts. To me, Bryan has always held a special place in my musical landscape as he kept bringing melodic, straightforward rock to the masses throughout the grunge-polluted nineties.

A CASUAL GUIDE TO THE MUSIC OF BRYAN ADAMS

I remember being pleased that the *Waking Up The Neighbours* album was so big at the same time Nirvana's hideously overrated *Nevermind* exploded. It meant there was still something out there that appealed to me (plus it was co-produced by Mutt Lange, who gave my childhood heroes Def Leppard their defining sound). I never connected to the Nirvana thing, and while 'Smells Like Teen Spirit' and the like bored me senseless, the sight of Bryan riding a giant Stratocaster like a Bucking Bronco in the video for 'Can't Stop This Thing We Started' was both hilarious and refreshing. Much like Bryan himself, really".

DEAN PEDLEY (*MIDLANDS ROCKS*): "It seems to be the poor relative of the back catalogue but I thought *Into The Fire* was a terrific album that has been unfairly forgotten over the years. It also marked a watershed in Adams' career being his last full length album pre- *Robin Hood*; the moment when his career took off in a whole other direction. This was when Adams was still taking risks and not simply trotting out sickly ballads ad infinitum that may have been lapped up by the masses but were lacking in depth and substance. Instead of love-sick lyrics *Into The Fire* had songs such as 'Native Son', inspired by the story of Chief Joseph of the Nez Perce ('nose pierced') tribe of Dakota. Another great song is 'Remembrance Day' which came to life when Jim Vallance visited the battlefields of northern France and sought out his great-uncle's grave.

I suppose the real reason this album is never mentioned much is the lack of a 'hit' single; it certainly wasn't *Reckless* 2 which was a strategy that so many of Adams peers were adopting in the '80s of basically rewriting a hit record time and time again. The closest thing to a love song is the dark and brooding 'Victim Of Love' but there is nothing on *Into The Fire* that sounds forced. He and Jim Vallance weren't thinking about chart success and sales figures when they wrote this record; something which Adams has been guilty of doing for much that has followed since".

JASON RITCHIE (*GET READY TO ROCK*): "*Kerrang!* magazine first tweaked my interest in Bryan Adams with the now classic *Reckless* album. One of those albums you still play now all these years later as Adams, along with writing partner Jim Vallance, had the knack of penning catchy and most importantly, memorable hard rock tunes. Every song could be performed live and even songs like 'Summer Of '69' which have been heard numerous times since still sound good. That opening guitar riff is so distinctive. Heck he even managed to give Tina Turner a run for her money on the duet 'It's Only Love'.

The three albums released before *Reckless* have mostly stood the test of time (his self-titled debut is not one I'd personally play now) and even a band as renowned as Uriah Heep did a sterling cover of an early

Adams/Vallance tune 'Lonely Nights'. After 1996's *18 Til I Die* I've not really listened to his music much as it has veered into the MOR area a little too much for my liking.

Live though he is still on top of his game. I saw him back in 1988 (I think!) at the recently opened GMEX in Manchester. He played for over two and half hours and the crowd were more exhausted than he was! I am pretty sure he would have carried on had there not been a venue curfew. An excellent live performer and his band are consummate musicians to, with long time guitarist Keith Scott and drummer Mickey Curry always on top form.

Bryan Adams appeal for me is the fact that either listening to his music or going to one of his concerts you can escape for a few hours and be guaranteed a good time. On album I doubt he can recapture those classic '80s years as they were very much a product of that time and place, however live he can still cut it and that's more than a lot of his contemporaries can do".

DAVE SCOTT (*FIREWORKS: THE MELODIC ROCK MAGAZINE*):
"I still remember how I first got into Bryan Adams. I was in my very early teens in the late eighties and had gone to Heathrow Airport with family to pick up another returning member.

Whilst we waited I took a stroll in the shops and even at this young age, I was very interested in music so it was off to HMV for me. As I perused the various albums on the racks, a song appeared over the shop PA and I was hooked from that moment; that song was 'Run To You'. That day I purchased a double cassette with *Cuts Like A Knife* and *Reckless* together (an item I still own to this day) and a few weeks later found *Into The Fire* in the family collections.

From these small cassettes, I have gone on to purchase every album in various formats and attended virtually every full tour (with one known exception) since the start of the nineties.

My favourite album?

This is a simple question for me: it is without doubt *Waking Up The Neighbours*. *Reckless* was the first album I bought and the one that got me into him in general and I will be the first to admit that it is full from start to finish with rock classics, but by the time I became a fan; it had already been out and so had the subsequent *Into The Fire*. The first album to come out after becoming a big fan was *Waking Up The Neighbours* and due to this it remains my sentimental favourite. I bought it the morning it came out and spent the whole day listening to it as I did for weeks after. I bought all the singles in all the formats as well as the album on CD and vinyl etc. Also the first official headline tour date I attended was one in support of this album. For all those factors it remains my personal favourite but it also extends to the tracks. *Reckless* has ten great tracks; *Waking Up The Neighbours* has sixteen so it wins out there too. 'House Arrest' and 'Hey Honey...I'm Packin' You In' are ripping live songs: 'Touch The Hand', 'Is Your Mama Gonna Miss Ya?', 'There Will Never Be Another Tonight' and 'Can't Stop This Thing We Started' are classic Bryan Adams rockers; there's the amusing lyrics of 'Is Your Mama Gonna Miss Ya' and 'If You Wanna Leave Me (Can I Come Too?)' yet in contrast 'Don't Drop That Bomb On Me' brings his political and environmental tendencies to the front and then there's the ballads. No one can forget THAT song but *Waking Up The Neighbours* also features 'All I Want Is You', 'Vanishing' and one of my Top 5 all-time songs in 'Thought I'd Died And Gone To Heaven'. On any front, for me, *Waking Up The Neighbours* has been and probably always will be my favourite Bryan Adams album and one of my all-time favourites to go with it".

RYAN SPARKS (*CLASSIC ROCK REVISITED*): "Many people probably don't realise that before Bryan Adams became the multi-million selling recording artist that he is today, he actually got his start writing songs for other artists with the help of partner and long-time collaborator Jim Vallance back in 1978. After a short stint handling lead vocals (as a young lad of only fifteen) for Canadian band Sweeny Todd on their second album *If Wishes Were Horses* (try finding a copy of that album today) released in 1977, the Adams / Vallance alliance began churning out songs for bands such as BTO, Prism and KISS, to name just a few.

Bryan's rise to superstardom as a solo artist was a gradual one that began inconspicuously enough with the release of his self-titled debut album in 1980. Over the course of the next three years Adams put out two more rock solid efforts (*You Want It You Got It* and *Cuts Like A Knife*) and logged countless miles on the road touring across North America with the likes of Foreigner, Loverboy, The Kinks and Journey. However, when album number four, *Reckless* was released in late 1984, you knew that things were about to really take off for the Kingston Ontario native. Six of the albums ten tracks were released as singles and by the summer of 1985 the album was still holding steady on the charts.

By the time I saw Bryan in concert in September of 1985 in Montréal, it was towards the end of the North American leg of the tour. I witnessed Adams and his tight band deliver the goods to a packed house that night as he tore through hit after hit from his seemingly endless arsenal of hits.

I never saw Adams live again. After that night, I didn't feel like I had to. In my mind he had finally arrived. He was no longer just Bryan Adams, Canadian artist from the West Coast. He was on the cusp of becoming so much more. He was about to go global".

A CASUAL GUIDE TO THE MUSIC OF BRYAN ADAMS

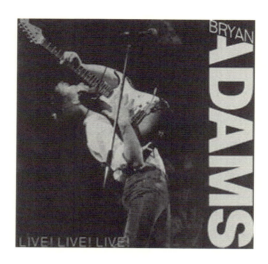

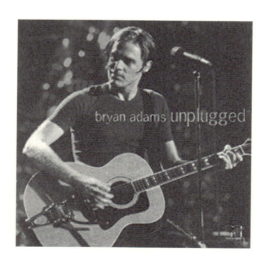

A CASUAL GUIDE TO THE MUSIC OF BRYAN ADAMS

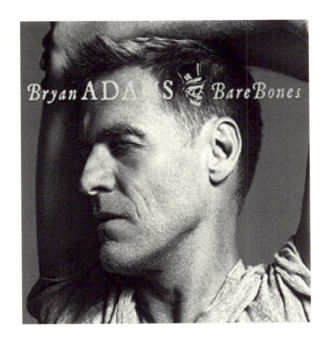

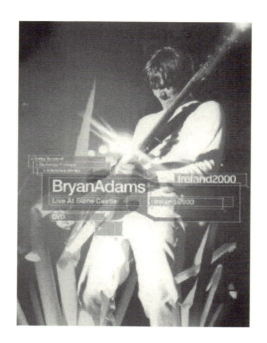

A CASUAL GUIDE TO THE MUSIC OF BRYAN ADAMS

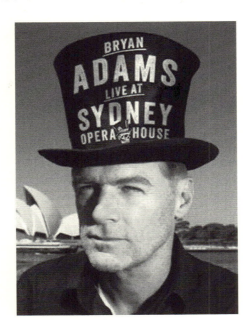

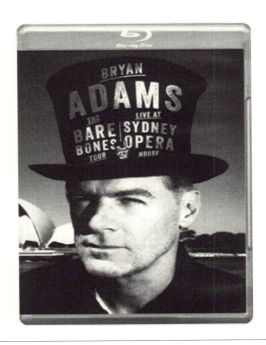

A CASUAL GUIDE TO THE MUSIC OF BRYAN ADAMS

DISCOGRAPHY

Here is a detailed discography of Bryan Adams' music. Though it is mostly focused on the UK/US releases there are some other regional releases included too.

STUDIO ALBUMS

BRYAN ADAMS

A&M, 1980

Hidin' From Love / Win Some, Lose Some / Wait And See / Give Me Your Love / Wastin' Time / Don't Ya Say It / Remember / State Of Mind / Try To See It My Way

YOU WANT IT, YOU GOT IT

A&M, 1981

Lonely Nights / One Good Reason / Don't Look Now / Coming Home / Fits Ya Good / Jealousy / Tonight / You Want It, You Got It / Last Chance / No One Makes It Right

CUTS LIKE A KNIFE

A&M, 1983

The Only One / Take Me Back / Straight From The Heart / Cuts Like A Knife / I'm Ready / What's It Gonna Be / Don't Leave Me Lonely / Let Him Know / The Best Was Yet To Come

RECKLESS

A&M, 1984

One Night Love Affair / She's Only Happy When She's Dancin' / Run To You / Heaven / Somebody / Summer Of '69 / Kids Wanna Rock / It's Only Love (with Tina Turner) / Long Gone / Ain't Gonna Cry

INTO THE FIRE

A&M, 1987

Heat Of The Night / Into The Fire / Victim Of Love / Another Day / Native Son / Only The Strong Survive / Rebel / Remembrance Day / Hearts On Fire / Home Again

WAKING UP THE NEIGHBOURS

A&M, 1991

Is Your Mama Gonna Miss Ya? / Hey Honey – I'm Packin' You In! / Can't Stop This Thing We Started / Thought I'd Died And Gone To Heaven / Not Guilty / Vanishing / House Arrest / Do I Have To Say The Words? / There Will Never Be Another Tonight / All I Want Is You /

Depend On Me / (Everything I Do) I Do It For You / If You Wanna Leave Me (Can I Come Too?) / Touch The Hand / Don't Drop That Bomb On Me

18 TIL I DIE

A&M, 1996

The Only Thing That Looks Good On Me Is You / Do To You / Let's Make A Night To Remember/ 18 Til I Die / Star / (I Wanna Be) Your Underwear / We're Gonna Win / I Think About You / I'll Always Be Right There / It Ain't A Party…If You Can't Come 'Round / Black Pearl / You're Still Beautiful To Me / Have You Ever Really Loved A Woman? / Hey Elvis*

Japanese bonus track

Australian tracklisting: The Only Thing That Looks Good On Me Is You / Do To You / Let's Make A Night To Remember / 18 Til I Die / Star / (I Wanna Be) Your Underwear / I Think About You / I'll Always Be Right There / It Ain't A Party If Ya Can't Come Round / Black Pearl / Have You Ever Really Loved A Woman? / I Finally Found Someone (with Barbra Streisand) / We're Gonna Win

ON A DAY LIKE TODAY

A&M, 1998

How Do Ya Feel Tonight / C'mon C'mon C'mon / Getaway / On A Day Like Today / Fearless / I'm A Lair / Cloud Number Nine / When You're Gone / Inside Out / If I Had You / Before The Night Is Over / I Don't Wanna Live Forever / Where Angels Fear To Tread / Lie To Me*

*European, South American and Australian bonus track

ROOM SERVICE

Polydor, 2004

Mercury, 2005 (US)

East Side Story / This Side Of Paradise / Not Romeo Not Juliet / Flying / She's A Little Too Good For Me / Open Road / Room Service / I Was Only Dreamin' / Right Back Where I Started From / Nowhere Fast / Why Do You Have To Be So Hard To Love? / Blessing In Disguise*

*British and Japanese bonus track

11

Polydor, 2008

Tonight We Have The Stars / I'd Thought I'd Seen Everything / I Ain't Losin' The Fight / Oxygen / We Found What We Were Looking For / Broken Wings / Somethin' To Believe In / Mysterious Ways / She's Got A Way / Flower Grown Wild / Walk On By / The Way Of The World*

*British and Japanese bonus track

A CASUAL GUIDE TO THE MUSIC OF BRYAN ADAMS

Deluxe edition bonus tracks: The Way Of The World / Saved / Miss American / She's Got A Way (Chicane Remix)

LIVE ALBUMS

LIVE! LIVE! LIVE!

A&M, 1994

She's Happy When She's Dancin' / It's Only Love / Cut's Like A Knife / Kids Wanna Rock / Hearts On Fire / Take Me Back / The Best Was Yet To Come / Heaven / Heat Of The Night / Run To You / One Night Love Affair / Long Gone / Summer Of '69 / Somebody / Walkin' After Midnight / I Fought The Law / Into The Fire

MTV UNPLUGGED

A&M, 1997

Summer Of '69 / Back To You / Cuts Like A Knife / I'm Ready / Fits Ya Good / When You Love Someone / 18 Til I Die / I Think About You / If Ya Wanna Be Bad – Ya Gotta Be Good / Let's Make A Night To Remember / The Only Thing That Looks Good On Me Is You / A Little Love / Heaven / I'll Always Be Right There

BARE BONES

Decca, 2010

You've Been A Friend To Me / Here I Am / I'm Ready / Let's Make A Night To Remember / It Ain't A Party If You Don't Come Round / (Everything I Do) I Do It For You / Cuts Like A Knife / Please Forgive Me / Summer Of '69 / Walk On By / Cloud Number Nine / It's Only Love / Heaven / The Right Place / The Way You Make Me Feel / The Only Thing That Looks Good On Me Is You / You're Still Beautiful To Me / Straight From The Heart / I Still Miss You…A Little Bit / All For Love

COMPILATIONS

HITS ON FIRE *(Japanese release)*
A&M, 1988

CD 1: Heat Of The Night / Into The Fire / Victim Of Love / Another Day / Native Son / Only The Strong Survive / Rebel / Remembrance Day / Hearts On Fire / Home Again

CD 2: Summer Of '69 / It's Only Love (with Tina Turner) / Straight From The Heart / Somebody / Heaven / This Time / Diana / Run To You / Cuts Like A Knife / Kids Wanna Rock (live) / Heaven (live) / One Night Love Affair

SO FAR SO GOOD

A&M, 1993

Summer Of '69 / Straight From The Heart / It's Only Love / Can't Stop This Thing We Started / Do I Have To Say The Words? / This Time / Run To You / Heaven / Cuts Like A Knife / (Everything I Do) I Do It For You / Somebody / Kids Wanna Rock / Heat Of The Night / Please Forgive*

*Previously unreleased

THE BEST OF ME

A&M, 1999

The Best Of Me / Can't Stop This Thing We Started / I'm Ready / Summer Of '69 / Let's Make A Night To Remember / All For Love / Have You Ever Really Loved A Woman? / Run To You / Cloud Number Nine / (Everything I Do) I Do It For You / Back To You / When You're Gone / Please Forgive Me / The Only Thing That Looks Good On Me Is You / Inside Out* /18 Til I Die

*Previously unreleased

Special Edition bonus disc (1999):

Summer Of '69 / Back To You / Can't Stop This Thing We Started / Have You Ever Really Loved A Woman? / Rock Steady

*All tracks are live from South Africa

Special Tour Edition bonus disc (2002):

Summer Of '69* / Back To You* / Can't Stop This Thing We Started* / Have You Ever Really Loved A Woman?* / Rock Steady* / Cloud Number Nine+ / I'm Ready+ / Cuts Like A Knife+

*Live from South Africa

+Live from Slane Castle

ANTHOLOGY

Polydor, 2005

International release:

CD 1: Remember / Lonely Nights / Straight From The Heart / Cuts Like A Knife / This Time / Run To You / Somebody / Heaven / Summer Of '69 / One Night Love Affair / It's Only Love (with Tina Turner) / Heat Of The Night / Hearts On Fire / (Everything I Do) I Do It For You / Can't Stop This Thing We Started / There Will Never Be Another Tonight / Thought I'd' Died And Gone To Heaven / All I Want Is You

CD 2: Please Forgive Me / All For Love (with Rod Stewart and Sting) / Have You Ever Really Loved A Woman? / Rock Steady (with Bonnie Raitt, live) / The Only Thing That Looks Good On Me Is You / Let's Make A Night To Remember / Star / Back To You (live) / I'm Ready (live) / One A Day Like Today / Cloud Number Nine (Chicane Remix) / Here I Am /

A CASUAL GUIDE TO THE MUSIC OF BRYAN ADAMS

This Side Of Paradise / Why Do You Have To Be So Hard To Love? / Open Road / 18 Til I Die (live) / When You're Gone (with Pamela Anderson) / So Far So Good

North American release:

CD 1: Remember / Lonely Nights / Straight From The Heart / Cuts Like A Knife / This Time / Run To You / Somebody / Heaven / Summer Of '69 / One Night Love Affair / It's Only Love (with Tina Turner) / Heat Of The Night / Hearts On Fire / (Everything I Do) I Do It For You / Can't Stop This Thing We Started / There Will Never Be Another Tonight / Thought I'd' Died And Gone To Heaven / The Best Of Me

CD 2: Please Forgive Me / All For Love (with Rod Stewart and Sting) / Have You Ever Really Loved A Woman? / Rock Steady (with Bonnie Raitt, live) / The Only Thing That Looks Good On Me Is You / Let's Make A Night To Remember / Star / Back To You (live) / I'm Ready (live) / One A Day Like Today / When You're Gone (with Mel C) / Cloud Number Nine (Chicane Remix) / The Best Of Me / Don't Give Up / Here I Am / Open Road / 18 Til I Die (live) / So Far So Good / I'm Not The Man You Think I Am

ICON *(US release)*

A&M, 2010

Summer Of '69 / Cuts Like A Knife / Can't Stop This Thing We Started / Run To You / Here I Am / Somebody / Cloud Number Nine / Have You Ever Really Loved A Woman? / The Only Thing That Looks Good On Me Is You / Straight From The Heart / (Everything I Do) I Do It For You

GREATEST HITS: AUSTRALIAN TOUR EDITION 2013 *(Australian release)*

Universal, 2013

CD 1: Summer Of '69 / (Everything I Do) I Do It For You / Heaven / When You're Gone / All For Love (live from the Royal Albert Hall) / Have You Ever Really Loved A Woman? (*Don Juan DeMarco* soundtrack version) / Run To You / Please Forgive Me / House Arrest (live from the Montreal Forum) / Flying (live from the Sydney Opera House) / The Only Thing That Looks Good On Me Is You / Can't Stop This Thing We Started / When You Love Someone (*MTV Unplugged* alternate take) / Cuts Like A Knife / Straight From The Heart (live from the Sydney Opera House) / Back To You (*MTV Unplugged* version) / 18 Til I Die

CD 2: Cloud Number Nine (Chicane Mix) / I'm Ready (MTV Unplugged version) / The Best Of Me / I'll Always Be Right There / You've Been A Friend To Me / Tonight In Babylon (live from the Sydney Opera House) /

Heat Of The Night / It's Only Love / This Time / Kids Wanna Rock / Somebody / Remember / One Night Love Affair / Hearts On Fire / There Will Never Be Another Tonight / Rock Steady (demo version) / All I Want Is You

SOUNDTRACKS

SPIRIT: STALLION OF THE CIMARRON
A&M, 2002

Here I Am (End Title) / I Will Always Return / You Can't Take Me / Get Off My Back (Super Trouper) / Brothers Under The Sun / Don't Let Me Go (Feat. Sarah McLachlan) / This Is Where I Belong / Here I Am / Sound The Bugle / Run Free / Homeland (Main Title) / Rain / The Long Road Back / Nothing I've Ever Known / I Will Always Return (Finale)

COLOUR ME KUBRICK
Universal, 2005

I'm Not The Man You Think I Am / It's All About Me / Rely On Me / Too Good To Be True / Gift Of Love

DVDs

MTV UNPLUGGED

A&M, 1997

Summer Of '69 / Cuts Like A Knife / I'm Ready / Back To You / Fits Ya Good / When You Love Someone / 18 Til I Die / I Think About You / If Ya Wanna Be Bad – Ya Gotta Be Good / Let's Make A Night To Remember / (I Wanna Be) Your Underwear / A Little Love / Can't Stop This Thing We Started / It Ain't A Party…If You Can't Come Round / Heaven / I'll Always Be Right There

LIVE AT SLANE CASTLE: IRELAND 2000

Universal, 2002

Back To You / 18 Til I Die / Can't Stop This Thing We Started / Summer Of '69 / It's Only Love / (Everything I Do) I Do It For You / Cuts Like A Knife / When You're Gone / She's Only Happy When She's Dancing / I'm Ready / Heaven / Blues Jam: If Ya Wanna Be Bad – Ya Gotta Be Good / Let's Make A Night To Remember / The Only Thing That Looks Good On Me Is You / Don't Give Up / Cloud Number Nine / Run To You / Please Forgive Me / Have You Ever Really Loved A Woman?* / Into The Fire* / Before The Night*

*Bonus tracks

LIVE AT THE BUDOKAN

A CASUAL GUIDE TO THE MUSIC OF BRYAN ADAMS

A&M, 2003

DVD: How Do Ya Feel Tonight / Back To You / 18 Til I Die / Can't Stop This Thing We Started / Summer Of '69 / It's Only Love / (Everything I Do) I Do It For You / Getaway / Cuts Like A Knife / When You're Gone / Have You Ever Really Loved A Woman? / Into The Fire / Remember / I'm Ready / Heaven / Blues Jam: If Ya Wanna Be Bad – Ya Gotta Be Good / Let's Make A Night To Remember / The Only Thing That Looks Good On Me Is You / Cloud Number Nine / Somebody / Run To You / Please Forgive Me / The Best Of Me / Fits Ya Good* / I Don't Wanna Live Forever* / Before The Night Is Over* / You're Still Beautiful To Me

Bonus tracks

CD: How Do Ya Feel Tonight / Can't Stop This Thing We Started / Summer Of '69 / Fits Ya Good / (Everything I Do) I Do It For You / Cuts Like A Knife / When You're Gone / Have You Ever Really Loved A Woman? / Getaway / Blues Jam: If Ya Wanna be Bad – Ya Gotta Be Good / Let's Make A Night To Remember / Cloud Number Nine / You're Still Beautiful To Me / Run To You / Please Forgive Me / The Best Of Me

LIVE IN LISBON

Universal, 2005

Room Service / Open Road / 18 Til I Die / Let's Make A Night To Remember / Can't Stop This Thing We Started / Kids Wanna Rock / Back To You / (Everything I Do) I Do It For You / Summer Of '69 / Cuts Like A Knife / When You're Gone / Not Romeo, Not Juliet / Heaven / It's Only Love / The Only Thing That Looks Good On Me Is You / Cloud Number Nine / Run To You / The Best Of Me / Flying / All For Love / Straight From The Heart / Room Service

LIVE AT SYDNEY OPERA HOUSE

Polydor, 2013

DVD: Run To You / Back To You / Here I Am / I'm Ready / This Time / Flying / Can't Stop This Thing We Started / Waiting On The '49 / In The Heat Of The Night / (Everything I Do) I Do It For You / Cuts Like A Knife / Please Forgive Me / Tonight In Babylon / Summer Of '69 / Walk On By / Heaven / The Right Place / The Only Thing That Looks Good On Me Is You / Somebody / You've Been A Friend To Me / When You're Gone / Have You Ever Really Loved A Woman? / I Still Miss You... A Little Bit / Straight From The Heart

CD: Run To You / Back To You / Here I Am / I'm Ready / This Time / Flying / Can't Stop This Thing We Started / Waiting On The '49 / In The Heat Of The Night / (Everything I Do) I Do It For You / Cuts Like A Knife

/ Tonight In Babylon / Summer Of '69 / Walk On By / Heaven / The Right Place / The Only Thing That Looks Good On Me Is You / You've Been A Friend To Me / When You're Gone / Have You Ever Really Loved A Woman? / I Still Miss You… A Little Bit / Straight From The Heart

SINGLES

'Let Me Take You Dancing' (1978)

'Give Me Your Love' (1980)

'Remember' (1980)

'Hidin' From Love' (1980)

'Coming Home' (1981)

'Fits Ya Good' (1981)

'Lonely Nights' (1982)

'Straight From The Heart' (1983)

'Cuts Like A Knife' (1983)

'This Time' (1983)

'Take Me Back' (1983)

'I'm Ready' (1983)

'The Only One' (1983)

'Run To You' (1984)

'Kids Wanna Rock' (1984)

'Somebody' (1985)

'Heaven' (1985)

'Summer Of '69' (1985)

'One Night Love Affair' (1985)

'It's Only Love' (with Tina Turner) (1985)

'Diana' (1985)

'Christmas Time' (1985)

'Het Of The Night' (1987)

'Hearts On Fire' (1987)

'Victim Of Love' (1987)

'Only The Strong Survive' (1987)

'Another Day' (1987)

'Run To You' (1989)

'Young Lust' (1990)

'(Everything I Do) I Do It For You' (1991)

'Can't Stop This Thing We Started' (1991)

'There Will Never Be Another Tonight' (1991)

'Thought I'd Died And Gone To Heaven' (1992)

'All I Want Is You' (1992)

'Do I Have To Say The Words?' (1992)

'Touch The Hand' (1992)

'Please Forgive Me' (1993)

'All For Love' (with Rod Stewart and Sting) (1993)

'Have You Ever Really Loved A Woman?' (1995)

'Rock Steady' (with Bonnie Raitt) (1995)

'The Only Thing That Looks Good On Me Is You' (1995)

'Let's Make A Night To Remember' (1996)

'Star' (1996)

'I Finally Found Someone' (with Barbara Streisand) (1996)

'18 Til I Die' (1996)

'Do To You' (1997)

'I'll Always Be Right There' (1997)

'Back To You' (1997)

'I'm Ready' (1998)

'On A Day Like Today' (1998)

'When You're Gone' (with Mel C) (1998)

'Cloud Number Nine' (1999)

'The Best Of Me' (1999)

'Don't Give Up' (Chicane feat. Bryan Adams) (2000)

'Inside Out' (2000)

'Here I Am' (2002)

'Me Voila' (2002)

'Open Road' (2004)

'Flying' (2004)

'Room Service' (2005)

'This Side Of Paradise' (2005)

'Why Do You Have To Be So Hard To Love?' (2005)

'So Far So Good' (2006)

'When You're Gone' (with Pamela Anderson) (2006)

'I Thought I'd Seen Everything' (2008)

'Tonight We Have The Stars' (2008)

'She's Got A Way' (2008)

'You've Been A Friend To Me' (2009)

'One World, One Flame' (2010)

'I Still Miss You…A Little Bit' (2010)

'Alberta Bound' (2001)

'Merry Christmas' (2011)

'Tonight In Babylon' (Loverush UK! Feta. Bryan Adams) (2012)

'After All' (Michel Buble feat. Bryan Adams) (2013)

A CASUAL GUIDE TO THE MUSIC OF BRYAN ADAMS

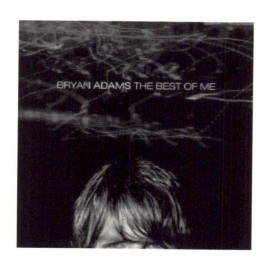

A CASUAL GUIDE TO THE MUSIC OF BRYAN ADAMS

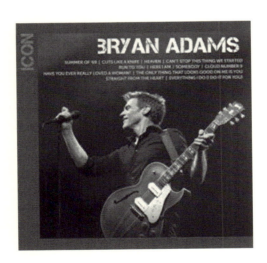

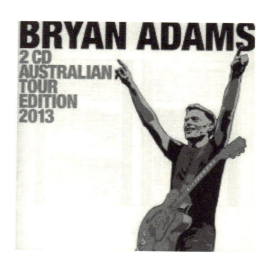

A CASUAL GUIDE TO THE MUSIC OF BRYAN ADAMS

NEIL DANIELS

AFTERWORD BY DAVE SCOTT
OF *FIREWORKS: THE MELODIC ROCK MAGAZINE*

I don't have one particular favourite concert from Bryan Adams as such. There are several that standout more than others for differing reasons but it wouldn't really be due to being just "a favourite performance". If push came to shove there's three that really stand out in my mind.

The most obvious would be my first ever concert at the Milton Keynes Bowl in 1991 when I went to watch Little Angels, Thunder, The Law, BA and ZZ Top. It was a seriously hot sunny day and a huge all-day outdoor gig; it was just perfect. I remember sitting on the bank looking at the stage, excited beyond belief that I was about to watch my hero live. Although I remember the day well, and his performance being great, I don't recall much specifically about his set which in part was probably due to him being on in the day light. I do remember him playing '(Everything I Do) I Do It For You' and it getting a hell of a reaction and then the very next day it became Number 1 where it stayed for those colossal sixteen weeks. Amazingly, it had only been knocked off the top spot for a week or two when I next saw him in November later that year.

The next year (July 1992) I attended another massive all-day effort with him at Wembley Stadium which was certainly another standout.

A CASUAL GUIDE TO THE MUSIC OF BRYAN ADAMS

This was partly due to it being the first gig I attended at the Stadium and the first time I had been on the famous pitch (I had previously been there for American football games). The day was opened by Little Angels again with Squeeze also part of the four band bill. It sticks in the mind particularly because in twenty-three years of gig going, I have never seen another show there where the stage was along the side not at one of the ends. It just made everything feel so much bigger and no matter where you stood you had a good view. His version of 'Run To You' was particularly special and you can still find video footage of it on YouTube. I also remember the riotous opening of 'House Arrest' and being blown away by 'Summer Of 69' and 'Thought I'd Died And Gone To Heaven'. The last real standout would be his *So Far So Good* Tour appearance at Wembley Arena in 1994.

Whilst driving up a friend and I were listening to his albums one after another and I remember us both saying how cool it would be to hear 'Lonely Nights' from his second album but he never plays anything that early. His opening song, 'Lonely Nights', and from there we knew this would be special.

He played for over three hours and about every song you could possibly want. I loathe all-seated gigs but this one was by far the best of that type I have ever been too.

Another moment I remember of that night is him playing Joe Cocker's 'When The Night Comes' and myself and friend clearly being the only two in our sight or hearing to be singing it. These three were special but there are so many other stand out gigs and live moments.

I once saw him three times in a week (twice at Wembley in three days) with different people and on the third night he bought out Tina Turner and did 'It's Only Love' together. There were the two Route Of The Kings concerts at Hyde Park in 1999 and 2002. The first was the inaugural year if memory serves me right, so it was all new. I remember going to the ever impressive food court and asking for the beer tent to be told with utter disgust at my question by the staff that "we at Route Of The Kings DO NOT have a Beer Tent...we have a Pimms, Wine and Champagne Tent". I will never forget roaming the event area watching old-school rockers strolling round with decanters, wine buckets/coolers and glasses of Pimms with utter bemusement; a very surreal moment.

There was also the on-off special event at Ashton Gate Stadium in Bristol in 2003 which was another chance to see him at a smaller event playing a selection of classics although I do recall we took hours to get back to our hotel afterwards being unable to find a taxi.

One abiding live memory comes from July 1996 when I saw him twice in a week, once in Huddersfield McAlpine Stadium then Wembley four days later.

A CASUAL GUIDE TO THE MUSIC OF BRYAN ADAMS

The Huddersfield gig was the last day of a five day trip up north to see friends that also included nights out and a day trip to Blackpool Pleasure Beach the day before so it's a memorable week all round.

I particularly recall near the end of the gig, the stage bathed in blue and him playing 'Let's Make A Night To Remember' and closing with 'Heaven' as the a cool breeze wafted over the crowd from behind the Stadium's open end behind the stage. It still makes me shiver now thinking about it as it was such an emotion moment.

The last time I saw him was at Bournemouth in Dec 2011 and we managed to get right to the front barrier and I have to admit it has quickly become a fourth favourite simply due to that. Prior the that the closest I have got was the few times where we walked in and spotted the small platform towards the rear which, being regular Bryan Adams goers, we know/knew means he would appear for a couple of songs at some point. It was always the first thing we looked for in the late nineties/early noughties. In summary, I have always found Bryan Adams to be one of the greatest live acts in the world.

He's engaging to listen to talking live, always plays the songs perfectly and knows how to work a crowd as well as anyone in the business; it doesn't hurt he has a plethora of catchy songs to choose from. I will always say, if you haven't seen Bryan Adams live you should, he really is one of the best ever!

I hope through my words you can sense a real love for Bryan Adams. Growing up in my teens and twenties, along with Whitesnake and Richie Sambora, he was one of my all-time three favourite acts but I'd be dishonest if I didn't state that that love has dulled a little, from an album point of view at least.

Growing up during those aforementioned decades, I was a completest; after everything I could get from releases to tours to merchandise.

As my twenties ended I got heavily into female-fronted symphonic metal and this love overtook my musical tastes generally and the likes of Def Leppard, Bon Jovi, Thunder and, to some extent, even Bryan Adams got relegated (Bryan Adams from the Top 3 although not the Top 5); that said Sambora and Snake remained where they are; make of that what you wish.

Reckless and *Waking Up The Neighbours* are as sensational today as they have always been and my love for them will never die. *Cuts Like A Knife* and *Into The Fire* are still classics in my eyes and I still love *18 Til I Die*.

In 1997 he released his critically acclaimed *Unplugged* album and a year later I was actually in Vancouver and purchased *On A Day Like Today* the week it was released.

A CASUAL GUIDE TO THE MUSIC OF BRYAN ADAMS

Whilst I enjoyed both albums, and appreciate hearing his classics in a different form on *Unplugged*, it was after *On A Day Like Today* where my enthusiasm started to wane (on the recorded material front from the height of adoration reached with the previous releases). It was here that he appeared to start following a mellower path that doesn't gel as well with me as his earlier work did.

Spirit did nothing to dispel this feeling and whilst I appreciate it was a soundtrack and enjoyed it in places (especially the ending track 'Here I Am') it continued the less "rocky" style that had become favoured by Bryan Adams. I was actually a big fan of *Room Service* which saw him return to his older sound with 'Open Road' and 'East Side Story' becoming two personal Bryan Adams favourites. But this didn't last long and I have to be brutally honest and say I thought his last album *11* was my least favourite of any of his full releases. For someone who can name every track on every other album in order and tell you about them, I can't tell you much at all about *11* bar the first couple of songs. It just didn't excite me and lacked the energy generally associated with Bryan Adams' songs. Don't get me wrong, it's still an above average album when compared to music in general; it just didn't excite me like so many of his others had.

Is that me getting older? Is that my changing taste changing my outlook? Has Bryan Adams mellowed just too far for my liking? It's probably yes, no and a little of that for all three and more.

His most recent release, *Bare Bones* is a bit of an exception to the rule. I really enjoyed it despite it being yet another acoustic offering but it was different to *Unplugged* due to him being effectively alone on stage. It hit the spot due mostly to the actual performance from the man himself but the audience were also lively and the songs were played at generally their original pace.

With all that said, whilst I may have cooled on his albums, my love for him as a live performer remains undiminished and I will always be striving to catch him live whenever he is in the UK. Whenever he tours with a full electric band, it's always an awesome evening and something I have never tired of.

Bryan Adams deserves a place at rock's top table and in rock history. Having been in the business for nearly thirty-five years, with several instantly recognisable classic hits in his locker and tours that continue to constantly sell out; there can be no denying his appeal and longevity. He has always had a knack of combining cracking riffs with infectious choruses that are just made to be played live.

I may not be as rabid about his albums as I once was but who knows what the next album will bring. Bryan Adams is just the sort of artist who is quite capable of producing something wonderful from nowhere that blows everyone away without warning.

I do so hope that will be the case; I desperately want a new Bryan Adams album that I can love like I did *Reckless* and *Waking Up The Neighbours*. But irrespective of it, Bryan Adams remains a rock star of the highest order who I hope continues to enthrall live audiences, of which I will be a part, for many years to come.

Dave Scott

Reviews Editor – ***Fireworks: The Melodic Rock Magazine***

Hampshire, July, 2014

NEIL DANIELS

A CASUAL GUIDE TO THE MUSIC OF BRYAN ADAMS

Photos by Dave Scott.

Photos by Dave Scott.

A CASUAL GUIDE TO THE MUSIC OF BRYAN ADAMS

APPENDECIES

A CASUAL GUIDE TO THE MUSIC OF BRYAN ADAMS

BIBLIOGRAPHY & SOURCES

The following books, magazines and websites were integral in the making of this book. I am deeply indebted to them all.

REFERENCE BOOKS

Betts, Graham. *Complete UK Hit Singles 1952-2005*. (London: Collins, 2005).

Betts, Graham. *Complete UK Hit Albums: 1956-2005*. (London: Collins, 2005).

Larkin, Colin. *The Virgin Encyclopaedia Of Rock*. (London: Virgin Books, 1999).

Roberts, David (Ed). *British Hit Singles & Albums*. (19th Edition) (London: Guinness World Records Ltd, 2006).

Strong, Martin C. *The Great Rock Discography*. (6th Edition) (London: Canongate, 2002).

MAGAZINES

Uncut

WEBSITES

http://blogcritics.org

http://cltampa.com

http://thecelebritycafe.com

http://jam.canoe.ca

http://web.archive.org

http://youhearthis.com

www.allmusic.com

www.animalliberationfront.com

www.bbc.co.uk

www.classicbands.com

www.dailymail.co.uk

www.entertainmentscene360.com

www.ew.com

www.examiner.com

www.ft.com

www.theguardian.com

www.masslive.com

www.maxtv.com.au

www.melodic.net

www.melodicrock.com

www.musicradar.com

www.nydailynews.com

www.people.com

www.popentertainment.com

www.reverbstreetpress.com

www.robertchristgau.com

www.rockunited.com

www.rollingstone.com

www.songfacts.com

www.songwriteruniverse.com

www.soundonsound.com

www.sputnikmusic.com

www.telegraph.co.uk

www.tntmagazine.in

www.usatoday.com

www.washingtonian.com

www.winnipegfreepress.com

www.zimbio.com

A CASUAL GUIDE TO THE MUSIC OF BRYAN ADAMS

ACKNOWLEDGEMENTS

Thank you to the following writers whose work I have quoted in this book. I am deeply indebted to them all. Their articles, reviews and interviews have provided invaluable insight into Bryan Adams' music.

Michelle Adamson, Gina Arnold, Bailey Brothers, June Bird, Joe Bosso, Robert Christgau, Mike DeGagne, Gabe Echazabal, Chuck Eddy, Dimitri Ehrlich, Rob Evans, Sophie Gilbert, Edna Gundersen, Nikk Gunns, Simon Hattenstone, Andrew Hawnt, Steve Hochman, James Hunter, Gary James, David Jenkins, Christ Jones, Dale Kawashima, Hester Lacey, Tom Lanham, Courtney Laura, Tracy May, Andrew McNeice, Dominick A. Miserandino, Donnie Moorehouse, John Newlin, Amy O'Brian, Derek Oliver, Andy Orrell, Dean Pedley, Jason Ritchie, Eduardo Rivadavia, Kaj Roth, Phil Roura, Dave Scott, Errol Somay, Ryan Sparks, Mark Stebbing, Darryl Sterdan, Adrian Thrills, Kimmo Toivonen, Deborah Wagner, Carl Wiser, Nathan Woods and Jen Zoratti.

A special thanks to Derek Oliver for his foreword and to Dave Scott, Ryan Sparks and Marie Skinner for providing photos of album covers, memorabilia and concerts.

A CASUAL GUIDE TO THE MUSIC OF BRYAN ADAMS

DISCLAIMER

The author gratefully acknowledges permission to quote and use references from the sources as referenced in the main text and repeated in the bibliography. Every quote and reference taken from selected sources is fully acknowledged in the main text and in the Bibliography & Sources. However, it has not been entirely possible to contact every copyright holder, but every effort has been made to contact all copyright holders and to clear reprint permissions from the list of sources. If notified, the publishers/author will be pleased to rectify any omission in future editions.

A CASUAL GUIDE TO THE MUSIC OF BRYAN ADAMS

ABOUT THE AUTHOR

NEIL DANIELS has written about rock and metal for a wide range of magazines, fanzines and websites. He has written over a dozen books on such artists as Judas Priest, Bon Jovi, Linkin Park, Journey, Neal Schon, Iron Maiden, You Me At Six, Metallica, AC/DC, Pantera, UFO, ZZ Top and Robert Plant. He also co-authored *Dawn Of The Metal Gods: My Life In Judas Priest And Heavy Metal* with original Judas Priest singer/co-founder Al Atkins. His third book on Judas Priest is the CD sized *Rock Landmarks – Judas Priest's British Steel*, published by Wymer.

His acclaimed series, *All Pens Blazing – A Rock And Heavy Metal Writer's Handbook Volumes I & II,* collects over a hundred original and exclusive interviews with some of the world's most famous rock and metal scribes. His second duel collection, *Rock 'N' Roll Mercenaries – Interviews With Rock Stars Volumes I & II*, compiles sixty interviews with many well-known rock stars and scribes. The former collections were republished via Createspace as *Rock 'N' Roll Sinners* while the latter books were republished in an omnibus edition titled, *Hard Rock Rebels – Talking With Rock Stars*.

A CASUAL GUIDE TO THE MUSIC OF BRYAN ADAMS

His Createspace books are *AOR Chronicles, Rock & Metal Chronicles, Hard Rock Rebels – Talking With Rock Stars, Rock 'N' Roll Sinners – Volumes I, II & III, Rock Bites, Love It Loud, Get Your Rock On – Melodic Rock Shots, Bang Your Head – Heavy Metal Shots, In A Dark Room – Exploits Of A Genre Fan* and the fictional rock 'n' roll novel, *It's My Life.*

His books have so far been translated into Brazilian, Bulgarian, Czech, Finnish, French, German, Italian, Japanese, Polish and Swedish with more foreign titles in the works.

His reviews, articles and interviews on rock music and pop culture have been published in *The Guardian, Classic Rock Presents AOR, Classic Rock Presents Let It Rock, Rock Sound, Record Collector, Big Cheese, Powerplay, Fireworks, MediaMagazine, Rocktopia.co.uk, Get Ready To Rock.com, Lucemfero.com, musicOMH.com, Ghostcultmag.com, Drowned In Sound.com, BBCNewsOnline.co.uk, Carling.com, Unbarred.co.uk* and *Planet Sound* on Channel4's Teletext service.

He has also written several sets of sleeve notes for Angel Air and BGO Records.

He can be found on Facebook, LinkedIn, Tumblr, Wordpress and Twitter. He has author pages on both Amazon US and UK sites. Further details can be found on Wikipedia.

More information is obtainable at his official website www.neildanielsbooks.com

He lives in the North West of England.

A CASUAL GUIDE TO THE MUSIC OF BRYAN ADAMS

PUBLISHED BOOKS BY NEIL DANIELS

MUSIC BIOGRAPHIES

The Story Of Judas Priest: Defenders Of The Faith

(Omnibus Press, 2007).

Robert Plant: Led Zeppelin, Jimmy Page And The Solo Years

(Independent Music Press, 2008).

Bon Jovi Encyclopaedia

(Chrome Dreams, 2009).

Dawn Of The Metal Gods: My Life In Judas Priest And Heavy Metal **(with Al Atkins)**

(Iron Pages, 2009).

Linkin Park – An Operator's Manual

(Chrome Dreams, 2009).

Don't Stop Believin' – The Untold Story Of Journey

(Omnibus Press, 2011).

Rock Landmarks: Judas Priest's British Steel

(Wymer Publishing, 2011).

Metallica – The Early Years And The Rise Of Metal

(Independent Music Press, 2012).

Iron Maiden – The Ultimate Unauthorised History Of The Beast

(Voyageur Press, 2012).

You Me At Six – Never Hold An Underdog Down

(Independent Music Press, 2012).

AC/DC – The Early Years With Bon Scott

(Independent Music Press, 2013).

Reinventing Metal – The True Story Of Pantera And The Tragically Short Life Of Dimebag Darrell

(Backbeat Books, 2013).

High Stakes & Dangerous Men – The UFO Story

(Soundcheck Books, 2013).

Beer Drinkers & Hell Raisers – A ZZ Top Guide

(Soundcheck Books, 2014).

Killers – The Origins Of Iron Maiden: 1975-1983

(Soundcheck Books, 2014).

Let It Rock – The Making Of Bon Jovi's Slippery When Wet

(Soundcheck Books, 2014).

CASUAL GUIDES

Electric World – A Casual Guide To The Music Of Journey's Neal Schon

(Createspace, 2014).

COLLECTED WORKS

All Pens Blazing: A Rock And Heavy Metal Writer's Handbook Volume I

(AuthorsOnline, 2009).

All Pens Blazing: A Rock And Heavy Metal Writer's Handbook Volume II

(AuthorsOnline, 2010).

Rock 'N' Roll Mercenaries – Interviews With Rock Stars Volume I

(AuthorsOnline, 2010).

Rock 'N' Roll Mercenaries – Interviews With Rock Stars Volume II

(AuthorsOnline, 2011).

CREATESPACE

AOR Chronicles – Volume 1

(Createspace, 2013).

Rock & Metal Chronicles – Volume 1

(Createspace, 2013).

Hard Rock Rebels – Talking With Rock Stars

(Createspace, 2013).

Rock 'N' Roll Sinners – Volume I

(Createspace, 2013).

Rock 'N' Roll Sinners – Volume II

(Createspace, 2013).

Rock 'N' Roll Sinners – Volume III

(Createspace, 2013).

Rock Bites

(Createspace, 2013).

Love It Loud

(Createspace, 2013).

Get Your Rock On – Melodic Rock Shots

(Createspace, 2013).

Bang Your Head – Heavy Metal Shots

(Createspace, 2013).

FILM/POP CULTURE

In A Dark Room – Exploits Of A Genre Fan

(Createspace, 2013).

FICTION

It's My Life – A (Fictional) Rock 'N' Roll Memoir

(Createspace, 2013).

PRAISE FOR THE AUTHOR'S PREVIOUS WORKS

"Neil Daniels is great on the early years of Brummie metal legends Judas Priest..."

- *Classic Rock* on **The Story Of Judas Priest: Defenders Of The Faith**

"'I've never reached the top...but I gave it a bloody good go!' says original Judas Priest singer Al Atkins in the introduction to his autobiography. With a foreword by Judas Priest bassist Ian Hill ... Metal Gods *covers the pre-fame years of the second-ever metal band in entertaining detail".*

- *Metal Hammer* on **Dawn Of The Metal Gods: My Life In Judas Priest And Heavy Metal**

"The book also has a curious appendices exploring – among other things – Percy's interest in folklore and mythology".

- *Mojo* on **Robert Plant: Led Zeppelin, Jimmy Page And The Solo Years**

"Prolific rock and metal author Neil Daniels does a very good job in detailing a veritable smorgasbord of the events, places, people, releases

and merchandises of the band, the writer displaying his customary attention to detail and enthusiasm for accuracy".

- *Record Collector* on **Bon Jovi Encyclopaedia**

"..in terms of writing, content and presentation I think it's probably his best... Linkin Park - An Operator's Manual *is an attractive book with black and white photos on every page".*

- *Fireworks* on **Linkin Park – An Operator's Manual**

"... the aggregate of this book is an at minimum interesting and at max fascinating read for any rock fan, 'cos you get the whole deal, the history of Sounds, Kerrang!, Metal Hammer, BW&BK, *all the mags, plus the mechanics of book writing, and more mainstream, who's a good interview and bad plus proof, crazy road stories...friggin' well all of this would be interesting to any rocker. Period".*

- *Bravewords.com* on **All Pens Blazing: A Rock And Heavy Metal Writer's Handbook Volume I**

"But once again, this rollercoaster ride through some of rock's back pages will bring a glow to the cheek, and perhaps even moistness to the mouth, of any self-respecting rock fan who has ever bought a music paper or mag since the 1970s".

- *Get Ready To Rock.com* on **All Pens Blazing: A Rock And Heavy Metal Writer's Handbook Volume II**

"These two volumes of interviews celebrate the art of rock journalism".

- *Classic Rock* on **All Pens Blazing: A Rock And Heavy Metal Writer's Handbook Volumes 1& 11**

"As a lone-time yet casual fan of the band, I found the band's story very interesting and quite surprising... I received the book on Thursday, used every possible opportunity to read it and finished it on Sunday. That's a recommendation if any".

- *Rock United.com* on **Don't Stop Believin' – The Untold Story Of Journey**

"With a track by track analysis, tour dates and photos from the period this is everything you needed to know about what is arguably Priest's finest thirty-odd minutes wrapped up into in one handy bite sized paperback at a budget price".

- *Sea Of Tranquility.org* on **Rock Landmarks – Judas Priest's British Steel**

"It's an insightful look at one of metal's most important bands, and though there have been many books written about them, Metallica have never seemed as easy to understand as after reading this".

- *Curled Up.com* on **Metallica – The Early Years And The Rise Of Metal**

"In all, Daniels has crafted a very high-level and easy read with Iron Maiden - The Ultimate Unauthorized History of the Beast, and top it all off, it's packaged expertly, prime for your coffee table, where Eddie's piercing eyes await".

- *Blistering.com* on **Iron Maiden – The Ultimate Unauthorised History Of The Beast**

"This book was a great read. 154 pages crammed with the wonderfully written story of You Me At Six… With some lovely photos and a very handy discography at the back, You Me At Six – Never Hold An Underdog Down is a must have for any YMAS fan".

- *Get Ready To Rock.com* on **You Me At Six – Never Hold An Underdog Down**

"Daniels style is engaging and covers in excellent detail the first six years of the band…Each chapter covers a year and Daniels provides great detail

on the various Australian vs. International pressings of the first few albums. It's very detailed and well researched".

- *Metal-Rules.com* on **AC/DC – The Early Years With Bon Scott**

"The tours, the music, the fun, the life, and the death, of one of the best metal acts of the '90s...it's all here. Nice job once again by Mr. Daniels".

- *Sea Of Tranquility.org* on **Reinventing Metal – The True Story Of Pantera And The Tragically Short Life Of Dimebag Darrell**

"Overall, I wouldn't hesitate to recommend this book to not only the diehards (who will snap it up anyway), but also those who want to delve just a little further than Michael Schenker, Phil Mogg (who emerges as quite the dictatorial figure in places), and the band's often horrendous choice of stage outfits!"

- *Classic Rock Society* on **High Stakes & Dangerous Men – The UFO Story**

"The book is an insight into the group's rise to fame, the funny times and their rise to become iconic bearded rocking heroes. I really enjoyed the section on ZZ Top trivia, there's funny and intriguing examples to make you smile and laugh out loud".

- *The Mayfair Mall Zine.com* on **Beer Drinkers & Hell Raisers – A ZZ Top Guide**

"This is a book for the superfan, to be honest. But for the superfan, it is a fantastic volume collecting a ton of information on a great player that you wouldn't be able to find in one place otherwise".

- *Music Tomes.com* on **Electric World – A Casual Guide To The Music Of Journey's Neal Schon**

"…if you thought you knew everything there was to know about Iron Maiden, then think again, as Daniels manages to turn up nugget after nugget of trivia and fact. This is a very rewarding read and I would wholeheartedly recommend this to any rock music fan, in fact buy it now and pack it away in your suitcase for your summer holiday read".

- *Planet Mosh.com* on **Killers – The Origins Of Iron Maiden: 1975-1983**

"Told in straightforward language and amazingly concise as for the time span it covers, Let It Rock: The Making of Bon Jovi's Slippery When Wet is a fine, solid work".

- *Hardrock Heaven* on **Let It Rock – The Making Of Bon Jovi's Slippery When Wet**

A CASUAL GUIDE TO THE MUSIC OF BRYAN ADAMS

ALSO AVAILABLE IN THIS SERIES:

ELECTRIC WORLD – A CASUAL GUIDE TO THE MUSIC OF JOURNEY'S NEAL SCHON

BY NEIL DANIELS
(CREATESPACE, 2014. ISBN: 1494710641)

Neal Schon is undoubtedly one of rock music's most versatile yet infuriatingly underrated guitarists. His work in the legendary multi-million selling AOR band Journey is universally known but what about his excellent solo albums and his other projects such as Bad English, HSAS, Hardline and Soul SirkUS, and not forgetting his many collaborations with the likes of Sammy Hagar, Paul Rodgers and Jan Hammer?

From the author of the acclaimed *Don't Stop Believin' – The Untold Story Of Journey*, *Electric World – A Casual Guide To The Music Of Journey's Neal Schon* is the first book to exclusively explore the music of the longest running member of one of the most successful American AOR bands of all time.

Electric World includes a foreword by Robert Fleischman, the original frontman of Journey, and exclusive interviews with such melodic rock heroes as Marco Mendoza, Jeff Scott Soto, Danny Vaughn, Glen Burtnik, Jimi Jamison and Ricky Phillips as well as a number of highly revered producers who have worked with Neal Schon such as Richie Zito and Mike Fraser. Also included are previously unpublished photos. *Electric World* is essential reading for Journey fans and AOR enthusiasts.

Electric World – A Casual Guide To The Music Of Journey's Neal Schon is a 6x9 344 page paperback and eBook.

WHAT THE PRESS SAID –

"It is a collection of pieces about Neal Schon and certainly for the avid Journey fan this book is a fascinating read and resource".
Jason Ritchie – *Get Ready To Rock (www.getreadytorock.co.uk)*

"The layout of the book is spacey and uncluttered and on the up side has a nice big font and lots of discography pages and line-up details (essential for the changing faces of Journey)…Once again, Daniels has prodigiously added to the AOR library".
Rob McKenzie – *Fireworks: The Melodic Rock Magazine*

"This is a very informative book regarding Schon and the maestro's career...Electric World is an interesting read and very informative book about the icon's status and history with and away from Journey".
Alison Bear – *The Mayfair Mall Zine (www.themayfairmallzine.com)*

"This is a book for the superfan, to be honest. But for the superfan, it is a fantastic volume collecting a ton of information on a great player that you wouldn't be able to find in one place otherwise".
Eric Banister – *Music Tomes (http://musictomes.com)*

"So this is written in a breezy, conversational style and not often looking deeper than chronological and celebratory narrative...this book brings you back to the music, which is what it's all about, really".
Steve Swift – *Powerplay: Rock & Metal Magazine*

"Even the most avid fan will no doubt find something to surprise them here, with Schon's work stretching from Michael Bolton and Joe Cocker to Paul Rodgers and Sammy Hagar. Daniels has pulled the whole thing together in one easy to digest guide that will be of considerable appeal to fans of Journey, Schon and the melodic rock scene in general".
Dean Pedley – *Sea Of Tranquility (www.seaoftranquility.org)*

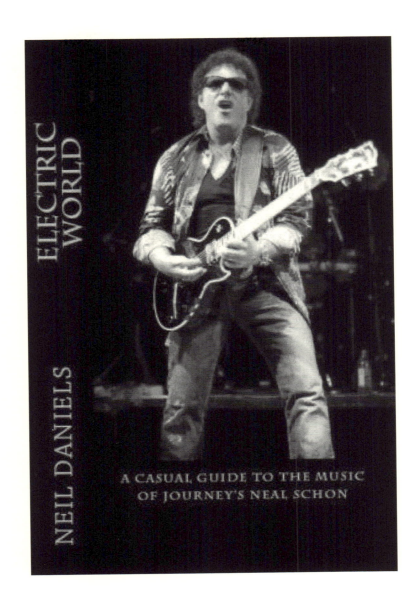

ALSO AVAILABLE FROM

NEIL DANIELS BOOKS

AOR CHRONICLES - VOLUME 1
Neil Daniels

Rock & Metal Chronicles - Volume 1
Neil Daniels

HARD ROCK REBELS - TALKING WITH ROCK STARS
Neil Daniels

Bang Your Head - Heavy Metal Shots
Neil Daniels

Get Your Rock On - Melodic Rock Shots
Neil Daniels

LOVE IT LOUD
Neil Daniels

ROCK 'N' ROLL SINNERS - VOLUME I
Neil Daniels

ROCK 'N' ROLL SINNERS - VOLUME II
Neil Daniels

ROCK 'N' ROLL SINNERS - VOLUME III
Neil Daniels

A CASUAL GUIDE TO THE MUSIC OF BRYAN ADAMS

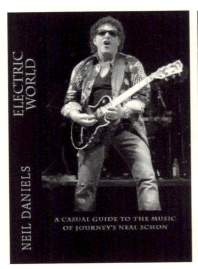

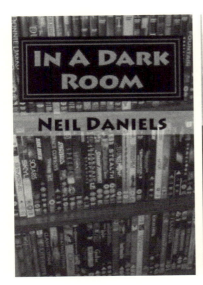
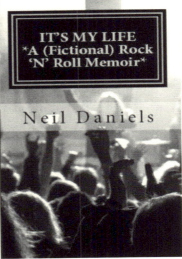

A CASUAL GUIDE TO THE MUSIC OF BRYAN ADAMS

YOU WANT IT YOU GOT IT

A CASUAL GUIDE TO THE MUSIC OF BRYAN ADAMS

NEIL DANIELS BOOKS

AUTHOR / CRITIC / MUSIC JOURNALIST / WRITER

QUALITY BOOKS ON ROCK & METAL MUSIC AND POP CULTURE

For details on Neil Daniels Books visit:

www.neildanielsbooks.com

Printed in Great Britain
by Amazon.co.uk, Ltd.,
Marston Gate.